Communications in Computer and Information Science 1531

More information about this series at https://link.springer.com/bookseries/7899

Inês Barbedo · Bárbara Barroso ·
Beatriz Legerén · Licínio Roque ·
João Paulo Sousa (Eds.)

Videogame Sciences and Arts

12th International Conference, VJ 2020
Mirandela, Portugal, November 26–28, 2020
Revised Selected Papers

 Springer

Editors
Inês Barbedo 🆔
Polytechnic Institute of Bragança
Mirandela, Portugal

Bárbara Barroso 🆔
Polytechnic Institute of Bragança
Mirandela, Portugal

Beatriz Legerén 🆔
Universidade de Vigo
Vigo, Spain

Licínio Roque 🆔
University of Coimbra
Coimbra, Portugal

João Paulo Sousa 🆔
Polytechnic Institute of Bragança
Mirandela, Portugal

ISSN 1865-0929   ISSN 1865-0937   (electronic)
Communications in Computer and Information Science
ISBN 978-3-030-95304-1   ISBN 978-3-030-95305-8   (eBook)
https://doi.org/10.1007/978-3-030-95305-8

This Springer imprint is published by the registered company Springer Nature Switzerland AG
The registered company address is: Gewerbestrasse 11, 6330 Cham, Switzerland

Preface

The 12th Conference on Videogame Sciences and Arts – Videojogos 2020 – was virtually held from Mirandela, Portugal, during November 26–28, 2020. Due to the COVID-19 pandemic context, activities were mostly conducted online, with participants from several countries. The conference was jointly organized by the School of Public Management, Communication and Tourism – Polytechnic Institute of Bragança (EsACT – IPB) and the Portuguese Society of Videogames Sciences (SPCV).

The annual conferences of the SPCV promote the scientific gathering of researchers and professionals in the expanded interdisciplinary field of videogames, usually held in Portugal. This year, 11 years after the first event, SPCV and the co-organizers adopted a full international profile with English as the main working language.

Indeed, both videogame academia and industry have been challenged over the past decade with the need to generate a confluence of different knowledge bases – from gameplay experience to art and design, in diverse materials and forms, AI, graphics, and other forms of computation and engineering, sound design, psychology, social and media studies, communication, and marketing, among others. In addition, games have been increasingly adopted as cultural artifacts in a hobbyist and cottage market and, therefore, presenting digitally mediated innovations in this popular but somewhat saturated global market is an increasingly demanding challenge.

As in previous editions, this conference gathered researchers and other professionals in the extended area of videogames, teachers and students, in a common forum to discuss videogame related topics and their impact on various aspects such as society, health, heritage, economy, or education. The goal of Videojogos is to promote the exchange of ideas, and share experiences and results in the areas of interest, through presentations, workshops, interactive demos, and panels.

From game design to the study of games in society, from player-centric to game-centric approaches, from interpretative studies to generative techniques, several works addressed key aspects of games and play, to bring forth updates to the body of knowledge and fundamental concepts in gameplay, balance and fairness, narrative fantasies, and flow experiences, which may lead to innovations in the way game environments are received in the gamer community.

In these proceedings, we open with a series of studies on relationships between the industry and society. Bruno Freitas, Ruth Contreras-Espinosa, and Pedro Correia address e-sports sponsorships and industry relationships with audiences. Flávio Nunes, Pedro Santos, Patrícia Romeiro, and Camila Pinto map the evolving trends in the Portuguese industry (2016–2020). Maitane Junguitu Dronda brings an insider's view on video games specialized media in the Basque language. Joana Mendes and Cristina Queirós address the industry old topic of "Crunch Time" and its effects like burnout and related job challenges in game development.

In the second section Néstor Jaimen Lamas addresses the perspective of game-based learning in science fiction. Then, Pedro Beça, Cláudia Ortet, Mónica Aresta, Rita

Santos, Ana Veloso, and Sofia Ribeiro bring a design instrument for supporting the construction of game narratives using a toolkit to game design (work was distinguished as the Best Paper).

The third section focuses on development techniques. Samuel Gomes, Tomás Alves, João Dias, and Carlos Martinho bring an innovative study of reward-mediated individual and altruistic behavior. Leading work in audio interface games, Gonçalo Baptista, Diogo Rato, and Rui Prada exploit the narrative scenario of "Interviewing a Virtual Suspect" as a basis for developing conversational game characters using Alexa. Pedro M. A. Fernandes, Pedro M. A. Inácio, Hugo Feliciano, and Nuno Fachada's study of evolutionary heuristics in the ColorShapeLinks board game competition. Augusto Dias, Juliano Foleiss, and Rui Pedro Lopes present a study of applicability of reinforcement learning in the context of tower defense games.

This book contains a selection of 10 papers from authors at reputed institutions in Portugal, Spain, and Brazil, which resulted from a selection of papers based on a double-blind peer review process, with a minimum of three reviews from an international panel, leading to a 40% acceptance rate. All these contributions address novel research and contribute developments or outcomes internationally relevant in the videogame research context, in a confluence of diverse scientific areas, such as multimedia, communication, computation and information technology, education, psychology, sociology, geography, media arts, marketing, etc.

This selection, obtained under very difficult conditions (conference submission, review, and organization at the height of the COVID-19 pandemic) confirms the decision to move the Videojogos conference out of the national domain, and towards an international platform reflecting global interests and relevance across diverse societies and geographies. This organizational change contributed to stabilize and further invest in the internationalization challenge assumed by the Portuguese Society of Videogames Sciences: to open up critically, and reflect and integrate views and ideas across international boundaries, towards a wider audience, whilst always striving for a holistic perspective, identifying trends and future directions. In this effort the bridge across Iberian and Latin-American countries is still notorious, although the evolution of the Program Committee leans towards an even more inclusive future profile of the conference organization.

To bridge the gap between industry and academia, representatives from industry were present and developed key roles in the organization of Videojogo 2020. Moreover, the conference included invited keynotes that addressed key aspects of game development and experience research.

Rui Craveirinha, from Player Research, addressed the theme "The Art of Play" with the following abstract: "What are video games? Why do we play them? What makes them feel so special to play? Is it - as everyone so fervently believes - that they're art? What even is art, anyway? Legend has it that I was born with a famicom controller… father tells me the cable served as the umbilical cord. It's thus no surprise that I spent most of my waking life feverishly musing on these deep questions, whether I was criticizing games for IGN or teaching Game Design at university. In this talk I will take you on a journey of the personal and the universal, retelling three distinct histories: the history of (video) games, from Chess to The Last of Us Part II; the history of aesthetics, from Plato to Dickie; and my own personal history, from playing famicom to analyzing player experience at Player Research. Together, these stories will intertwine in a way that might just answer all those questions. My answers can surprise, provoke, and, on the rarest of occasions, may even provide true insight. By the end, I hope to have at least convinced you of why video games are a wondrous medium which state-of-the-art theories and tools often downplay in terms of their sheer complexity, novelty... and beauty."

Oscar García Pañella, from ENTI-UB and a senior consultant at Cookie Box, addressed the theme "Seeking presence through virtuality – applying gamification to support the memorable experiences we deserve" with the following abstract: "We are still confined. Both physically and mentally, one or another or both depending on our specific context. And we are human beings and thus in need of social interaction, fantasy experimentation, true storytelling, and memorable challenges. We people love to explore, socialize, communicate, share, help, achieve ... and we need to feel engaged while doing so. Even more if using virtual devices for the majority of our communications. And because we are the users, we should be at the center of any design. Therefore, is there a science that can help us all to achieve the correct creation of valuable remote and/or hybrid experiences? Can we learn to design in a way that extracts the best opportunities from our current situation by allowing us to keep our networking alive while maintaining rigor and guaranteeing fun (and seriousness)? How can we expect to adapt ourselves to the "new" transmedia means available if not designing from both the experiential and memorable views? Welcome to the playing realms of motivational design and gamification!"

We would like to thank all the members of the scientific board for their contributions to guarantee and deliver the highest scientific quality, allowing the outstanding relevance of this book. We would also like to thank the program chairs (interactive, poster, and workshops) and the organization team for all their dedication and efforts in the organization, an extremely important contribution for the overall success of the Videojogos 2020 conference.

Finally, we would like to thank the Polytechnic Institute of Bragança (EsACT Mirandela) for hosting the event, and the Portuguese Society of Videogames Sciences for the organizational support and the publication of an additional volume of interactive works and works in progress, with a selection that did not meet the criteria for the full paper selection.

November 2020

Inês Barbedo
Bárbara Barroso
Beatriz Legerén
Licínio Roque
João Paulo Sousa

Organization

General Chairs

Inês Barbedo	Polytechnic Institute of Bragança, Portugal
João Paulo Sousa	Polytechnic Institute of Bragança, Portugal
Beatriz Legerén	University of Vigo, Spain

Program Committee Chairs

Bárbara Barroso	Polytechnic Institute of Bragança, Portugal
Licínio Roque	University of Coimbra, Portugal

Poster/Works in Progress Chairs

Jorge Palinhos	Polytechnic Institute of Bragança, Portugal
Markus Wiemker	HFT Stuttgart, Germany
Belén Mainer Blanco	Francisco de Vitoria University, Spain

Interactive Chairs

Carlos Casimiro Costa	Polytechnic Institute of Bragança, Portugal
Tanja Korhonen	Kajaani University of Applied Sciences, Finland
Jeferson Valadares	Doppio Games, Portugal/Brazil

Workshops Chairs

Rogério Azevedo Gomes	Polytechnic Institute of Bragança, Portugal
Rogério Tavares	Federal University of Rio Grande do Norte, Brazil

Local Organization Chair

António Mourão	Polytechnic Institute of Bragança, Portugal

Local Organization

André Monteiro	Polytechnic Institute of Bragança, Portugal
António Silva	Polytechnic Institute of Bragança, Portugal
Diogo Barbosa	Polytechnic Institute of Bragança, Portugal
Francisco Almeida	Polytechnic Institute of Bragança, Portugal
Francisco Pinto	Polytechnic Institute of Bragança, Portugal
Gabriel Batista	Polytechnic Institute of Bragança, Portugal
Gonçalo Oliveira	Polytechnic Institute of Bragança, Portugal

Gonçalo Pinto	Polytechnic Institute of Bragança, Portugal
Mário Costa	Polytechnic Institute of Bragança, Portugal
Marlon Faria	Polytechnic Institute of Bragança, Portugal
Paulo Brito	Polytechnic Institute of Bragança, Portugal
Rafael Batista	Polytechnic Institute of Bragança, Portugal

Design and Development

Carlos Casimiro Costa	Polytechnic Institute of Bragança, Portugal
Bárbara Barroso	Polytechnic Institute of Bragança, Portugal
Arlindo Santos	Polytechnic Institute of Bragança, Portugal
Ferdinando Silva	Polytechnic Institute of Bragança, Portugal
André Moreira	Polytechnic Institute of Bragança, Portugal
Andreia Pacheco	Polytechnic Institute of Bragança, Portugal
Hugo Fortes	Polytechnic Institute of Bragança, Portugal
Inês Silva	Polytechnic Institute of Bragança, Portugal
Luís Lopes	Polytechnic Institute of Bragança, Portugal

Steering Committee

Directive Board of the Portuguese Society for Videogame Sciences

Program Committee

Abel Gomes	University of Beira Interior, Portugal
Adérito Fernandes Marcos	Open University, Portugal
Alexis Blanchet	Université Sorbonne Nouvelle, France
Ana Amélia Carvalho	University of Coimbra, Portugal
Ana Lúcia Pinto	Polytechnic Institute of Bragança, Portugal
Ana Veloso	University of Aveiro, Portugal
André Neves	Federal University of Pernambuco, Brazil
António Coelho	University of Porto, Portugal
Antonio José Planells	University of Pompeu Fabra, Spain
Antonio Pena	University of Vigo, Spain
Bárbara Barroso	Polytechnic Institute of Bragança, Portugal
Beatriz Legerén	University of Vigo, Spain
Belén Mainer Blanco	Francisco de Vitoria University, Spain
Bruno Giesteira	University of Porto, Portugal
Bruno Silva	European University, Portugal
Carla Ganito	Catholic University of Portugal, Portugal
Carlos Casimiro Costa	Polytechnic Institute of Bragança, Portugal
Carlos Martinho	University of Lisbon, Portugal
Carlos Santos	University of Aveiro, Portugal
Christian Roth	University of Utrecht, The Netherlands
Ciro Martins	ESTG Águeda, Portugal

Conceição Costa	Lusófona University, Portugal
Cristiano Max	Universidade Feevale, Brazil
Daniela Karine Ramos	Federal University of Santa Catarina, Brazil
Diego Perez-Liebana	Queen Mary University of London, UK
Diogo Gomes	University of Aveiro, Portugal
Duarte Duque	Polytechnic Institute of Cávado and Ave, Portugal
Emmanoel Ferreira	Fluminense Federal University, Brazil
Esteban Clua	Fluminense Federal University, Brazil
Euridice Cabañes	Arsgames, Mexico
Eva Oliveira	Polytechnic Institute of Cávado and Ave, Portugal
Fanny Barnabé	University of Liège, Belgium
Filipe Luz	Lusófona University, Portugal
Filipe Penicheiro	University of Coimbra, Portugal
Fotis Liarokapis	Technical University of Cyprus, Cyprus
Francisco Javier Gayo Santacecilia	U-tad, Spain
Frutuoso Silva	University of Beira Interior, Portugal
Gabriel Fernandes	Federal Institute of Rio de Janeiro, Brazil
Gustavo Reis	Polytechnic Institute of Leiria, Portugal
Héctor Quintián	University of A Coruña, Spain
Ido Iurgel	Hochschule Rhein-Waal, Germany
Inês Barbedo	Polytechnic Institute of Bragança, Portugal
Jeferson Valadares	Doppio Games, Portugal/Brazil
Jesus Torres	University of La Laguna, Spain
João Dias	University of Lisbon, Portugal
João Jacob	University of Porto, Portugal
João Paulo Sousa	Polytechnic Institute of Bragança, Portugal
João Victor Gomide	FUMEC University, Brazil
Jorge Martins Rosa	New University of Lisbon, Portugal
Jorge Palinhos	Polytechnic Institute of Bragança, Portugal
José Luís Rolle	University of A Coruña, Spain
Juan Albino Mendez Perez	University of La Laguna, Spain
Leonel Morgado	Open University, Portugal
Licínio Roque	University of Coimbra, Portugal
Liliana Costa	University of Aveiro, Portugal
Lynn Alves	Federal University of Bahia, Brazil
Marçal Mora Cantallops	University of Alcalá, Spain
Marcos Antón	Complutense University, Spain
Mário Vairinhos	University of Aveiro, Portugal
Markus Wiemker	HFT Stuttgart, Germany
Marta Nuñez	Universitat Jaume I de Castellón, Spain
Mercedes García Betegon	U-tad, Spain
Micael Sousa	University of Coimbra, Portugal
Michel Santorum	Tequila Works, Spain
Miguel Carvalhais	University of Porto, Portugal
Nelson Zagalo	University of Aveiro, Portugal

Contents

Esports Sponsorships: The Double-Edged Sword Effect of Having a Very Vocal Audience

Bruno Duarte Abreu Freitas[1]([email]) [iD], Ruth Sofia Contreras-Espinosa[1] [iD],
and Pedro Álvaro Pereira Correia[2] [iD]

[1] University of Vic - Central University of Catalonia, Barcelona, Spain
`brunoduarte.abreu@uvic.cat`
[2] University of Madeira, Funchal, Portugal

Abstract. Esports fans have been known for being heavy consumers of competitive gaming content and for being digital natives who love to comment about esports on numerous social platforms. This has attracted various sponsors interested in capitalizing in this social buzz. However, there have been signs that this high vocality can in fact heavily damage several sponsors. Hence, this research aimed to determine if esports fans' high vocality is a benefit and/or a risk to these sponsors. To achieve this, we adopted a qualitative exploratory design to interview, via digital platforms, 10 esports sponsorship experts. In total, we interviewed two endemic and three non-endemic esports sponsors and five marketing agencies with experience in esports sponsorships. They were sampled via a nonprobability purposive heterogeneous method and were reached via the companies' website contact sections. Data were analyzed with the assistance of NVivo 10. The overall results showed that all experts agreed that this high vocality can both benefit and damage esports sponsors. The uniformity in the answers showed that this element is not a greater benefit or risk to a particular type of esports sponsor. Ergo we considered that the high vocality of esports fans is a double-edged sword. This study is necessary because, despite esports' massive growth, this field has received scant scientific attention, with the specific areas of esports marketing and esports sponsorships being even more severely overlooked. Besides, from a business standpoint, the findings are highly significant for every sponsor looking to better comprehend esports and its fanbase.

Keywords: Esports · Sponsorships · Consumer behavior · Market analysis · Marketing

1 Introduction

Electronic sports (esports) are professionally organized videogame competitions where highly skilled gamers – commonly dubbed as *pro-players* or *pro-gamers* – compete [1] to earn prestige, money, prizes, etc. [2]. Just like water sports, esports is a collective term. That is, it is comprised of a large number of disciplines (i.e. videogames) and a competition can feature various tournaments of different games [3]. The competitions are divided into numerous tiers of professionalism [4], including amateur [5], high-tier

© Springer Nature Switzerland AG 2022
I. Barbedo et al. (Eds.): VJ 2020, CCIS 1531, pp. 1–14, 2022.
https://doi.org/10.1007/978-3-030-95305-8_1

amateur, and professional [6]. While most low tier competitions are held via the internet, with players competing from their residences [7], high-tier and popular tournaments are carried out in large spaces, like major arenas, where enthusiastic fans gather to personally watch their favorite pro-gamers compete in eye-catching matches that are also streamed over the internet [8].

Although esports only started gaining popularity in the beginning of the 2010s [3], they have, in a very short time [1], become a worldwide phenomenon [9]. Competitive gaming has already been recognized as an official sport in South Korea and several western countries are following suit [9]. Esports has only now reached this threshold because information and communication technologies just recently reached a state where streaming and social networking have become accessible to the general consumer [10]. Now, competitive gaming is, not only the world's fastest-growing sport [11], but also one of the fastest-growing industries overall [4]. Their high economic significance [1] allied with their large international reach [12] and popularity has attracted the attention of numerous consumer brands who now view it as an important marketing channel [13]. Ergo, just in 2016, over 600 sponsorship[1] contracts were signed [1]. Among the most popular esports sponsors, there are brands like Microsoft, Samsung, Red Bull [15], Vodafone, Coca-Cola [3], Paris Saint-German, Nissan, Google, Manchester City, Audi, and Sony [1].

There are numerous benefits that are attracting sponsors to esports. One of the main benefits sponsors seek to obtain is an increased brand awareness [3]. Specifically, sponsors have been attracted by esports' massive audience [3]. In 2020, it is estimated there were 495 million esports fans and this number is expected to increase to 646 million by 2023 [16, 17], a value much higher than the whole NFL audience and in line with the fan-bases of other popular sports [1]. And this audience has been increasing between 10.4% and 12.3% per year [16]. Competitive gaming is filling out entire football stadiums [3] and receiving higher viewership levels than the highest profile events in sports. For instance, while 1.7 million people tuned in to Watch-ESPN to see Germany face the United States in the 2014 Football World Championship [13], 46 million people tuned into Twitch and YouTube to watch the Intel Extreme Masters esports tournament in Katowice [18]. Another benefit sponsors seek to attain is increased sales [4]. It has been found that esports fans have an above-average income [3] and are compulsive buyers, early adopters [4], and influencers of the buying behavior of technology-related products [3]. Furthermore, this market was estimated to be worth 1.34 billion US dollars in 2020 [19] and this value has been increasing roughly 9.7% per year [20]. An additional benefit esports sponsors obtain is a surprising general acceptance of sponsorships [3]. Unlike other industries where sponsorship activities are under the risk of being perceived as unwanted or intrusive [21], esports fans have shown to understand that esports cannot survive without sponsors [3]. Hence, there is a general positivism around esports sponsorships [22]. This dependency also gives rise to the benefit of it being much cheaper to sponsor esports than most sports [4] and to the benefit of the brands that sponsor

---

[1] According to the International Chamber of Commerce [14], a sponsorship is a mutually beneficial commercial partnership where an entity (i.e. a sponsor) provides funding, or another type of support, to a second entity (i.e. the sponsored party) to acquire the right to associate its image, brands, and products with the second entity through promotional activations.

esports acquiring an improved brand image. This latter benefit arises from the fact that fans perceive esports sponsors as supporters of the fragile industry they love [1].

Besides these appealing benefits, it has also been assumed that esports fans' intimate connection with digital media can have a significant positive effect on esports sponsors [1]. This is because their main demographics – millennials and generation Z – are known for having a very high online affinity. Esports fans and gamers have come together in multiple e-communities that reside in various social media, forums, websites, and other channels like in-game guilds and clans. These communities have developed into an ecosystem where any gamer can very swiftly meet, communicate, and share esports content [3]. In essence, esports fans can be perceived as digital natives [1, 3]. Unlike the preconceptions of old, which saw gamers as friendless lone introverts who would shy away from any kind of social contact [23], this audience, in fact, actively seeks social interactions and loves meeting new people and belonging to a community [24].

The truth is that esports fans are extremely vocal [25, 26]. They love to interact with one another and even with the general gaming fans who might not be into esports [1]. Data shows that 51% of esports fans chat with other gamers on a regular basis and that 69% make use of social platforms while gaming [26]. The main promoter of this high vocality is esports' intimate connection with the internet. Almost all esports related social activity happens on social networks [27]. Streams of esports events feature integrated chats that allow fans to communicate and interact with one another and even with the streamers themselves. This means that fans actively participate in the event and are immersed in the experience [28]. Another element that catapults this high vocality is the fans' love for esports [4]. The fans are very deeply engaged and highly attached and passionate about esports [3]. During offline tournaments, it is common for esports fans to wear their favorite team's apparel, cheer, and wave flags [13]. A study found that 63.4% of fans consume 5 to 10 h of esports content per week and another one concluded that roughly two-thirds of esports fans consider esports watching to be their most important hobby, and some even see it as their passion [3]. This high involvement makes them a very valuable consumer target from a marketing perspective [3, 29]. In fact, one of the main reasons why sponsors have entered esports is because they want to reach this passionate audience [30]. The attractiveness of this audience is also catapulted by the fact that roughly one-fifth of esports fans enjoy following esports sponsors activities on social platforms [22]. It is because of this that some brands prefer to sponsor a pro-player that is very social and constantly interacts with its audience over someone who is a better player [31]. A pro-gamer who is very social will also promote his sponsors more to his hundreds of thousands of enthusiastic fans [13].

In essence, esports fans love to use a plethora of social platforms (e.g. Facebook, Twitter, Instagram, Snapchat, and Reddit) to talk about esports and this heavy communication creates a buzz that significantly increases the sponsors' presence in social and digital media [22]. However, having a very vocal audience can also bring about some risks to sponsors, like being much more susceptible to backlashes [4] and extreme criticism [13]. Because of the issues of this ambivalent dichotomy, this research aimed to determine if esports fans' high vocality is a benefit and/or a risk to esports sponsors. In other words, this study sought to answer the research question: How does esports fans' high vocality affect esports sponsors? This study is necessary because, despite esports' massive growth [29], this field has received scant scientific attention [29, 32, 33, 34], with the specific area of esports marketing [28, 29, 35] and esports sponsorships being even more severely overlooked [3, 36, 37, 38].

2 Literature Review

2.1 The Benefits of Having a Very Vocal Audience

Multiple sponsors have entered the esports scene with the intent of capitalizing on the fans' high vocality and were very successful. For example, when sponsoring the professional team Astralis, Audi noticed that just the media exposure caused by the fans' buzz on social media was worth more than 10 times what the brand had initially invested. And this was just during one edition of the DreamHack and ELEAGUE tournaments. Even more impressive was that 82% of the buzz had come from only the ELEAGUE event. This was largely because Astralis had a terrific performance and won the tournament [22].

Esports sponsors have been able to reach millions of fans on social media like Facebook and Twitter on a daily basis [13]. This is mainly because of esports fans' constant use of social platforms to talk about gaming and esports [22]. Instead of just reading tournament or pro-player posts, or information about them, fans prefer to show their support in much more visible ways, like through social media. This, in turn, creates a lot of buzz and exposure around esports entities and the brands that sponsor them [4]. Whenever fans witness an exciting moment in a match they immediately comment about it on various chats and forums. This propagates the excitement, which in turn boosts esports' viewership levels [25]. All of the hype that the propagation of these messages creates is very attractive for sponsors as it provides them with a large reach in a hyped-up environment. By reaching fans when their emotions are exponentially high, sponsors also benefit from positive brand image transfer [4].

This aspect of positive association has been given further relevance by a joint research between the consultancy agency Accesso and the Asociación Española de Videojuegos (AEVI) which revealed that 98% of all esports-related communications on social media have a positive sentiment (i.e. acceptance, support, gratitude, etc.) and just 2% portray negative emotions. This is a highly significant contrast to the common communication dynamics of general social media which show much higher toxicity. According to AEVI, this abundance of positive emotions is one of the primary reasons why so many sponsors have entered the esports scene [27].

Since these fans like to talk about esports and all aspects related to it [4], this also means that they are important influencers of their social environments. Their capability of influencing other people's buying behavior means, that by sponsoring esports, brands are reaching, not only the core fan-base, but also a much larger consumer group [13]. On average, an esports fan influences the buying behavior of technology products of at least four family members or friends [3, 13]. Interestingly, some sponsors have indicated that what they seek the most in esports is not a boost in sales. Instead, they wish to build their brand with the help of this community's enthusiastic buzz [31]. And, as the esports community grows, they are becoming increasingly more vocal, which in turn creates even more opportunities for brands [4]. Based on these arguments, we propose the following:

H_{1a}: The high vocality of esports fans is a benefit to esports sponsors.

2.2 The Risks of Having a Very Vocal Audience

Esports fans are extremely critical [13]. So much so that any sponsor who communicates with them without a profound esports knowledge is under the risk of being heavily criticized [26]. For instance, fans will frown upon any sponsor that seems to only be interested in making a sale [37]. The critical nature of esports fans means that brands must enter esports with caution since poor activations can result in severe brand damage and negative ROIs [13]. Because of this, it is vital that sponsors learn about the esports culture and its fans [22, 26]. Still, even sponsors with esports knowledge can be heavily criticized. For instance, Bud Light decided to create a pro-team called Bud Light All-Stars by asking fans to choose pro-players from a selection they presented [1]. The act of involving esports fans with sponsorship activations and allowing them to participate has shown to increase their overall satisfaction with the brand [4]. However, the sponsor was strongly criticized and even accused of only being interested in acquiring popular brand ambassadors rather than strictly building a strong team [1].

The high vocality is also affecting esports women. There have been several instances of women facing brutal online chats with asinine messages that range from scary to outright rage [4]. Kelly "kellyMILKIES" Ong, is one of the many examples of female pro-players who even received photoshopped pictures with her face on naked bodies or images showing her being raped or murdered [39]. This discredits the professionalism of the esports scene and puts the brands that sponsor it in a risky situation [4].

Esports fans can be quite brutal and rude with their language. One study that analyzed various esports-related chats, forums, and websites found a plethora of tweets and posts containing homophobia, misogyny, harassment, transphobia, general hate, and even death and rape threats, as well as threats of physical violence [40]. However, it is not only the fans that use inappropriate language. There have been pro-gamers who did the same, like Jake "orb" Sklarew and Greg "IdrA" Fields, who started using offensive language. This led a large number of fans to organize campaigns and complain to their sponsors. The fan criticism was so voracious that the sponsors had to fire the pro-players [39].

Esports fans can easily generate backlashes against anything they disagree with. An example of this occurred in 2014 during the finals of *CS:GO* at DreamHack. During the event, team Fnatic exploited a glitch that allowed them to easily shoot all adversaries in the entire map and win the match. However, after being caught, instead of pleading guilty, Fnatic accused the opposing team of also exploiting glitches. This resulted in DreamHack announcing that the finals had to be repeated. But this created a lot of controversies and led the very vocal fans to inundate several social channels with heavy backlashes against Fnatic and its sponsors. The fan backlash was so strong that Fnatic was forced to give up the tournament [4]. According to Ströh [3], these fan backlashes are a threat to esports sponsors.

Also, whenever a sponsored pro-player loses a match, the sponsor will suffer from negative brand image transfer and lose credibility [31], especially because of the negative comments that will spread over the internet about the pro-player's defeat and how the sponsors may be partially to blame [4]. In the same vein, poorly organized tournaments will result in the events' main sponsor being heavily criticized. For instance, during the 2007 grand finals of the World Cyber Games – whose main sponsor was Samsung – the fans saw Song "Stork" Byung Goo exploiting a glitch to win the game, but the referees did not notice this, and before the referees became aware of the situation, Stork's opponent gave up the match. This generated a severe uproar among the fans and heavy commentary among esports reporters. The discussion became so profound that it caught the attention of multiple South Korean general media, which led to a further spreading of the issues caused in a major tournament sponsored by Samsung. As of today, the event is still recalled as an aberration. Another way that the sponsor can be heavily criticized is when the products they bring to the event malfunction. For example, there have been several instances of sponsor monitors turning off during esports matches and, unfortunately, these incidents are not forgotten. They go on to be deeply criticized by the fans on various online communities. A different issue that goes on to be heavily discussed by fans and can damage the sponsor's image is when a tournament does not give the winners the prize money. This is an issue that has become commonplace in several esports tournaments and has put the image of both the tournament organizers and sponsors at risk [41]. All of these issues led us to propose the following:

H_{1b}: The high vocality of esports fans is a risk to esports sponsors.

3 Methodology

To reach the goal of this research, we adopted a qualitative exploratory design. An overt stance was used in a non-contrived setting and in a cross-sectional time horizon. The sample was composed of 10 esports sponsorship experts. Specifically, two endemic esports sponsors (EESs), three non-endemic esports sponsors (NEESs), and five marketing agencies (MAs) that worked in the field of esports sponsorships. Only one expert in esports sponsorships was contacted for each of these organizations. These individuals were sampled via a nonprobability purposive expert heterogeneous methodology. Specifically, there was a deliberate selection of a diverse group of individuals with large amounts of knowledge and experience in esports sponsorships. To ensure these organizations had been working with esports sponsorships for a relevant amount of time, only organizations with at least two years of experience in esports sponsorships were contacted. The sample was reached by contacting the organization's marketing departments or directors via the companies' website contact sections or by sending them an email to the addresses in the aforementioned sections. Both the unit of analysis and the unit of observation was the organization.

The empirical data was gathered via an interview with each expert. In the interviews, besides asking questions on the company's characteristics, the experts were asked to answer the open-ended question "How beneficial and/or harmful do you believe the esports fans' high vocality can be for esports sponsors?" The interviews were mostly held on Skype, with some being conducted on other digital platforms (i.e. Microsoft Teams and Zoom) at the request of some interviewees. Prior to starting the interviews, the questionnaire was pretested between 14 April 2019 and 21 May 2019 on nine individuals with expertise in the areas of management, marketing, and general scientific research. Afterwards, the empirical data collection began on 15 August 2019 and ended on 12 December 2019. The data were analyzed with the assistance of the computer software NVivo 10. To comply with the confidentiality norms of social research, all sensitive data that could allow the research subjects to be identified (e.g. company name, exact year of foundation, etc.) were either modified or not included in the study.

Regarding the specifics of the sample members, EES1 was founded in the 1980s and operates internationally in the gaming retail industry. EES1 has been sponsoring esports for two years, has sponsored roughly nine esports entities, and has been connected to roughly seven esports videogames. The interviewee's position within EES1 was of head of partnerships.

EES2 was founded in the 2010s and operates internationally in the gaming chair industry. EES2 has been sponsoring esports for roughly seven years, has sponsored roughly 44 esports entities, and has been connected to roughly 41 esports videogames. The interviewee's position within EES2 was of country general manager in the United Kingdom, Brazil, Spain, and Portugal.

NEES1 was founded in the 2010s and operates internationally in the industry of consumer electronics (with special focus on smartphones, phone cases, and headphones). NEES1 has been sponsoring esports for three years, has sponsored roughly four esports entities, and has been connected to roughly 11 esports videogames. The interviewee's position within NEES1 was of head of global brand partnerships.

NEES2 was founded in the 1920s and operates nationally (i.e. in the USA) in the insurance industry. NEES2 has been sponsoring esports for two years, has sponsored roughly 12 esports entities, and has been connected to roughly six esports videogames. The interviewee's position within NEES2 was of director of marketing, media, and sponsorships.

NEES3 was founded in the 1990s and operates nationally (i.e. in the USA) in the craft beer and brewing industry. NEES3 has been sponsoring esports for two years, has sponsored roughly 14 esports entities, and has been connected to roughly six esports videogames. The interviewee's position within NEES3 was of community, partnerships, sponsorships, and major events manager.

MA1 was founded in the 2000s and operates internationally by exclusively providing marketing advice in the esports and videogames sector. MA1 has been connected to esports for approximately 11 years, has assisted roughly 100 esports sponsors, and has been connected to roughly 35 esports videogames. The interviewee's position within MA1 was of founder and director.

MA2 was founded in the 2010s and operates internationally by exclusively providing marketing advice in the esports and videogames sector. MA2 has been connected to esports for two years, has assisted roughly 40 esports sponsors, and has been connected to roughly 39 esports videogames. The interviewee's position within MA2 was of founder and director.

MA3 was founded in the 2010s and operates internationally by exclusively providing marketing advice in the esports and videogames sector. MA3 has been connected to esports for two years, has assisted roughly 100 esports sponsors, and has been connected to roughly nine esports videogames. The interviewee's position within MA3 was of founder and director.

MA4 was founded in the 1990s and operates internationally by providing marketing advice in various sectors, including esports and videogames. MA4 has been connected to esports for approximately four years, has assisted roughly 15 esports sponsors, and has been connected to roughly 15 esports videogames. The interviewee's position within MA4 was of account director and esports specialist.

MA5 was founded in the 2000s and operates internationally by exclusively providing marketing advice in the esports and videogames sector. MA5 has been connected to esports for approximately six years, has assisted roughly 50 esports sponsors, and has been connected to roughly 43 esports videogames. The interviewee's position within MA5 was of senior market analyst and esports specialist.

4 Results and Discussion

The overall results confirmed H_{1a} and H_{1b}, meaning that the high vocality of esports fans is both a benefit and a risk to esports sponsors. The empirical data showed that all experts agreed that this high vocality can benefit sponsors and that all also agreed that it can damage them. This showed that there was no difference in opinions between the different members of the sample (i.e. EESs, NEESs, and MAs). Hence, the data did not point to this being a greater benefit or risk to either endemic or nonendemic sponsors. Ergo we considered that the high vocality of esports fans is a double-edged sword for all types of esports sponsors.

The experts provided very insightful commentaries. Regarding the benefits of high vocality, it was stressed that fans will show highly positive reactions when brands correctly carry out a sponsorship. Amongst the favorable responses, MA5 stated that brands can expect "really big positive language and positive sentiment… in online communities, on social media, etc…. It's an improved brand image". This shows how the high vocality of a happy community that makes heavy use of digital platforms can significantly benefit the sponsor. Similarly, MA4 indicated that there was a tournament sponsored by DHL that the fans loved so much that they even started chanting "DHL! DHL! DHL!" at the stadium. This shows an unprecedented love for brands that carry out well-coordinated sponsorships. The response of MA4 is pretty much in line with EES1, who provided one of the most relevant responses from all the experts by stating that the esports fan-base shows more support and love for the sponsors than the communities of almost any other sport or sponsored area.

A number of experts indicated some suggestions and tactics to correctly activate the sponsorships and make the most out of the positive aspects of this high vocality. Particularly, it was stressed that sponsors should thoroughly study esports (MA3) and the fan-base before signing any sort of contract (MA5). It is imperative that the sponsorship is relevant (MA3) and authentic (NEES1). Specifically, the promotions must resonate with fans (MA5) and show that the brand cares and is passionate about esports and that it truly wants to be a part of competitive gaming (NEES1).

Concerning the dangers of high vocality, the experts pointed out that sponsorships must be very carefully planned as some brand actions can easily result in extremely negative fan reactions. Amongst these, EES1 gave examples of fans who boycotted esports sponsors. EES2, NEES2, NEES3, and MA4 noted that there have been several instances of sponsors who suffered from strong verbal backlashes from the fan-base on multiple social media and forums. Similarly, MA2 indicated that some esports communities were even completely outraged at the sponsors. MA1 and MA2 stressed that a large number of fans can become so angry at some sponsors that they will do all they can to damage the brand and its image. According to MA2, one example of this is through the creation of damaging memes based on the sponsor or on people that work for the brand. MA2 also made the very important remark that, because this audience is deeply socially connected, they will never forget the sponsors' wrongdoings or mistakes. They will do all they can do to burn the sponsors' image to the ground and will not give up that easily or so soon. NEES1, NEES2, and MA2 reported that the negative communications about the sponsor will possibly spread and lead both the esports fans and some of the general gaming audience to develop a resistance to the sponsorship actions of the brands they are not happy with.

Several experts indicated some of the sponsor actions that lead fans to spread negative communications about the brand. These include: communicating or presenting views that are not in line with the community's general opinion (EES1), being unauthentic (NEES1), poorly activating a sponsorship or advertisement (NEES1; MA1; MA2; MA5), showing a lack of knowledge about esports and its fan-base and a lack of interest in learning about them, and appearing like an overly commercial brand whose only goal is the selling of products and services (MA3). Figure 1 shows how esports fans generally react to correct and poor sponsorship activations.

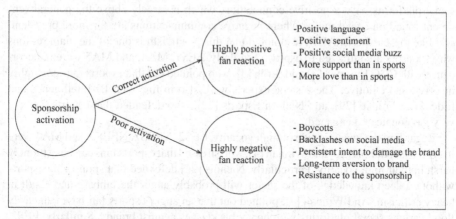

Fig. 1. Esports fans' reactions to correct and poor sponsorship activations

EES2 also pointed out that, sometimes, it is very difficult for a sponsor to not anger the fan-base and be negatively affected by their high vocality. EES2 gave the example that whenever a sponsored player is involved in a controversy, the brand must cancel the sponsorship to avoid being seen as a supporter of disrespectful behavior by the fans. However, while this will calm some fans, it may also lead others to criticize the sponsor for canceling a sponsorship for minor reasons and contributing to esports' high volatility. In a similar example, EES2 also reported that fans often heavily criticize brands that sponsor female pro-gamers by saying that the brand is exploiting women by using them to call the attention of male esports fans. However, whenever a brand refuses to sponsor a female pro-gamer, the brand is also harshly criticized for being misogynistic. Figure 2 illustrates these two examples of when a negative fan reactions cannot be avoided.

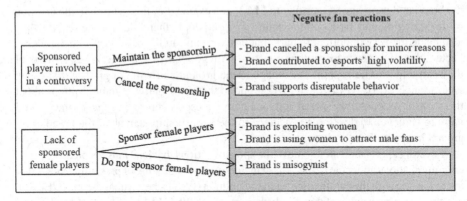

Fig. 2. Instances where negative fan reactions cannot be avoided

A large number of similarities were found between the empirical data and the literature. In terms of the benefits of high vocality, EES1 and MA5 were somewhat in sync with AEVI [27], who indicated that 98% of esports-related communications on social platforms have a positive connotation, which is largely above the general sentiment found on social media where negative communications are far more prevalent. Just like these experts, AEVI also noted that this positivism is one of the main reasons why sponsors are attracted to esports. Similarly, EES1, MA4, and MA5 were in accordance with CGC Europe [13] and Ströh [3], who pointed out that esports fans are highly involved and emotive. These same experts were also in line with BI Intelligence and Elder [12], Franke [29], and Nielsen Esports [22], who defended that esports fans are very passionate and engaged.

Regarding the negative side of high vocality, EES2, NEES2, NEES3, and MA4 were in sync with Nichols [26] and Winnan [4], who stressed that esports fans can be extremely harsh in their high vocality. Particularly, Nichols [26] defended that sponsoring esports without a deep knowledge of the sector will probably anger the fanbase and result in heavy criticism. And Winnan [4], pointed out that an angry esports fan-base can easily flood various social platforms with heavy backlashes against brands. Similarly, EES2, NEES2, NEES3, MA1, MA2, and MA4 were in line with CGC Europe [13], who reported how exceedingly critical esports fans can be.

4.1 Managerial Implications

From a business standpoint, the findings are highly significant for every brand with an interest in sponsoring esports as well as for those looking to comprehend how the esports fans' high vocality might positively or negatively affect them. It is imperative that esports sponsors come to terms with the fact that they are entering a field of highly passionate individuals and that they will be touching on something deeply loved by a large and hyper socially-connected audience. Hence, and as stressed by MA1, depending on how the sponsorship is conducted, "the audience will love you or hate you." Despite there being a large fan-base and reports of an abundance of positive sentiment on esports-related fan communications, sponsors have to understand that, as MA4 indicated, "the advantage of having a highly engaged community also brings the disadvantage of having a very protective community." Just like EES2 indicated, the fans can "make your social media increase and decrease as they please, both in terms of followers and in making posts go viral, etc." In essence, the highly vocally of the esports fan-base, which is promoted by their high engagement, passion, and heavy use of social media, has a strong influence over the sponsorships' success and the brands' ROIs; like brand image, awareness, and sales.

The fans' heavy commentary means that it is vital that brands interested in sponsoring esports carefully study it before engaging with the scene. The sponsors with a high understanding of the fan-base and general competitive gaming will be much more likely to activate sponsorships that are in sync with the community's desires and will be able to naturally integrate into the scene. As a result, the fan-base will have a highly positive response to the sponsors' activations. Ergo, taking the time to thoroughly figure out esports and its fan-base, focusing on relevancy and authenticity, showing love and interest for competitive gaming, and performing activations that truly resonate with fans are key elements to benefit from the fan-base's high vocality and reap ROIs like positive fan sentiment, improved brand image, brand loyalty, and increased sales and awareness.

Notwithstanding the aforementioned tactics, sponsors must still be wary. Particularly, brands must make sure their advertisements do not contradict nor offend the fan-base opinions and views and avoid being seen as self-centered sponsors whose only interest is selling. Furthermore, sponsors must be careful so that angered esports fans do not flood their social media pages with hateful comments. Firstly, because this may lead the general consumers to develop negative impressions of the brand due to seeing a large number of people angry at the brand. And secondly, if people outside the esports sphere take notice of esports fans' occasional rude language and views, the image of the brands that sponsor this industry may be heavily damaged. Although rude and disrespectful language might be commonplace in social media, if the general consumer becomes aware that a brand is supporting what is supposed to be a professional industry where both pro-gamers and fans make use of offensive language, it may negatively affect their views of the brand.

It is also advised to thoroughly ponder which entities the brand should start or stop sponsoring. As EES2 indicated, several sponsors will be faced with situations where basically any brand decision will anger some fans. EES2 also stressed that, while sports entities are mostly safe to sponsor, esports entities must always be closely watched by their sponsors due to their youth, professional inexperience, and higher chance of engaging in disreputable behavior. Hence, esports sponsors must not associate themselves with entities that may put them in delicate situations. Ergo, it is imperative to know which esports entities are the safest to sponsor. This again shows the importance of carefully studying esports prior to engaging in any kind of sponsorship.

The high vocality of this audience has attracted a large number of sponsors but, as EES1 defends, can also repel some. The harshness of this high vocality was wholly pictured by MA1 when he noted that the heavy use of the internet and social media by the fans and the existence of platforms like Reddit mean that the community will never forget bad or poor sponsor conducts or activations and will not easily give up on attacking the sponsor. Similarly, MA2 also stated that "the internet never forgets… once you screw up with the internet it's really tough and expensive to get back on track. You might as well drop esports for a year and then come back." These problems highlight the importance of cautiously developing sponsorships that use this high vocality as a tool to benefit the sponsor instead of harming it.

5   Limitations and Future Research

This study was limited by the lack of scientific research and reliable literature on the specific topic of esports sponsorships, esports marketing, and on the behavior of esports fans. Another limitation was the difficulty to contact and interview a large number of experts in esports sponsorships, which resulted in the lack of an equal number of EESs, NEESs, and MAs. This could have biased the results to more strongly represent the views of MAs – which comprised half of the sample – and less the opinions of EESs and NEESs.

Future studies should build upon the findings of this research and focus on analyzing how effective are this study's suggested tactics to maximize and mitigate the benefits and risks of having a very vocal audience, respectively. It would also be interesting to verify if there are more esports sponsors being benefited or damaged by this high vocality and to interview more sponsors and marketing agencies in search of more specific examples of how and why some sponsors are greatly benefited by this high vocality while others are severely damaged by it.

References

1. Shabir, N.: Esports: The Complete Guide 17/18: A Guide for Gamers, Teams, Organisations and Other Entities in, or Looking to Get into the Space. Independently Published, Wroclaw (2017)
2. Mooney, C.: Inside the E-Sports Industry. Norwood House Press, North Mankato, MN (2018)
3. Ströh, J.H.A.: The eSports Market and eSports Sponsoring. Tectum Verlag, Marburg (2017)
4. Winnan, C.D.: An Entrepreneur's Guide to the Exploding World of eSports: Understanding the Commercial Significance of Counter-Strike, League of Legends and DotA 2. The Borderland Press, Kindle eBook (2016)
5. Hamari, J., Sjöblom, M.: What is eSports and why do people watch it? Internet Res. **27**(2), 211–232 (2017). https://doi.org/10.1108/IntR-04-2016-0085
6. SuperData. Esports Courtside: Playmakers of 2017 (December 2017). http://strivespo nsorship.com/wpcontent/uploads/2017/12/SuperData-2017-Esports-Market-Brief.pdf. Accessed 6 Apr 2018
7. Stein, V., Scholz, T.M.: Sky is the limit – eSports as entrepreneurial innovator for media management. In: Jesus, S.N., Pinto, P. (Eds.) Proceedings of the International Congress on Interdisciplinarity in Social and Human Sciences, pp. 622–631. University of Algarve, Faro, CIEO – Research Centre for Spatial and Organizational Dynamics (2016). http://hdl.handle. net/10400.1/9888

8. Gifford, C.: Gaming Record Breakers. Carlton Books Limited, London (2017)
9. Davenport, T., Mansar, S., Reijers, H., Rosemann, M.: Preface. In: Eder, J., Dustdar, S. (eds.) BPM 2006. LNCS, vol. 4103, pp. 3–4. Springer, Heidelberg (2006). https://doi.org/10.1007/11837862_1
10. Carter, M., Gibbs, M.: eSports in EVE online: Skullduggery, fair play and acceptability in an unbounded competition. In: Yannakakis, G.N., Aarseth, E., Jørgensen, K., Lester, J.C. (Eds.) Proceedings of the 8th International Conference on the Foundations of Digital Games, pp. 47–54. Society for the Advancement of the Science of Digital Games, Chania (2013)
11. Sylvester, R., Rennie, P.: The world's fastest-growing sport: maximizing the economic success of esports whilst balancing regulatory concerns and ensuring the protection of those involved. Gaming Law Rev. **21**(8), 625–629 (2017). https://doi.org/10.1089/glr2.2017.21811
12. BI Intelligence, Elder, R.: The eSports competitive video gaming market continues to grow revenues & attract investors. Business Insider, 15 March 2017. http://www.businessinsider.com/esports-market-growth-ready-formainstream-2017-3. Accessed 22 Feb 2018
13. CGC Europe (2015). Marketing Channel eSports – How to get the attention of young adults? http://docplayer.net/12867287-Marketing-channelesports-how-to-get-the-attention-of-young-adults.html. Accessed 19 Jan 2018
14. International Chamber of Commerce. Consolidated ICC Code of Advertising and Marketing Communications Practice (2011). http://www.codescentre.com/downloads.aspx
15. Funk, D.C., Pizzo, A.D., Baker, B.J.: eSport management: embracing eSport education and research opportunities. Sport Manage. Rev. **21**(1), 7–13 (2018). https://doi.org/10.1016/j.smr.2017.07.008
16. Newzoo. Key Numbers (2020). https://newzoo.com/keynumbers/. Accessed 13 July 2020
17. Statista. eSports audience size worldwide from 2018 to 2023, by type of viewers (April 2020). https://www.statista.com/statistics/490480/globalsports-audience-size-viewer-type/. Accessed 13 July 2020
18. Statista. Number of unique viewers of selected eSports tournaments worldwide from 2012 to 2017 (in millions), January 2018. https://www.statista.com/statistics/507491/esports-tournaments-by-number-viewers-global/. Accessed 16 Mar 2018
19. Pannekeet, J.: Newzoo: Global Esports Economy Will Top $1 Billion for the First Time in 2019, (12 February 2019). https://newzoo.com/insights/articles/newzoo-global-esports-economy-will-top-1-billion-forthe-first-time-in-2019/. Accessed 14 July 2019
20. SuperData. European eSports Conference Brief, February 2017. http://strivesponsorship.com/wp-content/uploads/2017/04/Superdata-2017-sportsmarket-brief.pdf. Accessed 16 Mar 2018
21. Crompton, J.: Benefits and risks associated with sponsorship of major events. Festiv. Manage. Event Tourism **2**(2), 65–74 (1994). https://doi.org/10.3727/106527094792292050
22. Nielsen Esports. The Esports playbook: maximizing your investment through understanding the fans. In: Pike, N., Master, S., (Eds.) (2017). http://www.nielsen.com/us/en/insights/reports/2017/the-esports-playbook-maximizinginvestment-through-understanding-the-fans.html
23. Newman, J.: Playing with Videogames. Routledge, Abingdon (2008)
24. Hilvert-Bruce, Z., Neill, J.T., Sjöblom, M., Hamari, J.: Social motivations of livestreaming viewer engagement on Twitch. Comput. Hum. Behav. **84**, 58–67 (2018). https://doi.org/10.1016/j.chb.2018.02.013
25. Ford, C.M.: Virtuosos on the screen: playing virtual characters like instruments in competitive super smash bros. Melee. In: CHI 2017 Proceedings of the 2017 CHI Conference on Human Factors in Computing Systems, pp. 1935–1948 (2017). https://doi.org/10.1145/3025453.3026053
26. Nichols, M.: Endemics vs non-endemics: eSports expanding its sponsorship horizons. European Sponsorship Association (2017). http://sponsorship.org/wpcontent/uploads/2017/08/Sportcals-Endemic-vs-Non-Endemics-eSports-expanding-itssponsorhip-horizons.pdf

27. AEVI. Libro blanco de los esports en España (2018). http://www.aevi.org.es/web/wp-con tent/uploads/2018/05/ES_libroblanco_online.pdf

28. Seo, Y.: Electronic sports: a new marketing landscape of the experience economy. J. Mark. Manag. **29**(13–14), 1542–1560 (2013). https://doi.org/10.1080/0267257X.2013.822906

29. Franke, T.: The perception of eSports - mainstream culture, real sport and marketisation. In: Hiltscher, J., Scholz, T.M., (Eds.) eSports Yearbook 2013/14, pp. 111–144. Norderstedt: Books on Demand GmbH (2015). http://esportsyearbook.com/eyb201314.pdf

30. Lee, D., Schoenstedt, L.J.: Comparison of eSports and traditional sports consumption motives. ICHPER-SD J. Res. **6**(2), 39–44 (2011). https://eric.ed.gov/?id=EJ954495

31. Pitkänen, J.: Value creation through sponsorship in electronic sports. Master thesis, Lappeen-ranta University of Technology, Lappeenranta (2015). http://www.doria.fi/handle/10024/104883

32. Faust, K., Meyer, J., Griffiths, M.D.: Competitive and professional gaming: discussing poten-tial benefits of scientific study. Int. J. Cyber Behav. Psychol. Learn. **3**(1), 67–77 (2013). https://doi.org/10.4018/ijcbpl.2013010106

33. Weiss, T., Schiele, S.: Virtual worlds in competitive contexts: analyzing eSports consumer needs. Electron. Mark. **23**(4), 307–316 (2013). https://doi.org/10.1007/s12525-013-0127-5

34. Lokhman, N., Karashchuk, O., Kornilova, O.: Analysis of eSports as a commercial activ-ity. Probl. Perspect. Manage. **16**(1), 207–213 (2018). https://doi.org/10.21511/ppm.16(1).2018.20

35. Burton, R.: Using eSports efficiently to enhance and extend brand perceptions. In: 15th Annual Sport Marketing Association Conference, Boston, MA, Novem-ber, 2017. https://static1.squarespace.com/static/54358491e4b0e09faedc4a1b/t/59d64d355 1a5842e17641a57/1507216693800/BURTON_RICK_FORMATTED.pdf

36. Cunningham, G.B., et al.: eSport: construct specifications and implications for sport management. Sport Manage. Rev. **21**(1), 1–6 (2018). https://doi.org/10.1016/j.smr.2017.11.002

37. Korpimies, S.: Sponsorships in eSports. (Bachelor thesis), Aalto University, Espoo (2017). http://urn.fi/URN:NBN:fi:aalto-201705114490

38. Hallmann, K., Giel, T.: eSports – competitive sports or recreational activity? Sport Manage. Rev. **21**(1), 14–20 (2018). https://doi.org/10.1016/j.smr.2017.07.011

39. Li, R.: Good Luck Have Fun: The Rise of eSports. Skyhorse Publishing, New York, NY (2016)

40. Menti, D.C., Araújo, D.C.: Violência de gênero contra mulheres no cenário dos eSports. Conexão - Comunicação e Cultura, **16**(31), 73–88 (2017). http://www.ucs.br/etc/revistas/index.php/conexao/article/view/4948

41. Taylor, T.L.: Raising the Stakes: E-Sports and the Professionalization of Computer Gaming. The MIT Press, Cambridge, MA (2012)

Recent Trends in the Portuguese Video Game Industry: 2016 – 2020

Flávio Nunes[1]([✉]) [iD], Pedro Santos[2] [iD], Patrícia Romeiro[3] [iD], and Camila Pinto[4] [iD]

[1] CECS – Universidade do Minho, Braga, Portugal
flavionunes@geografia.uminho.pt
[2] INESC-ID and Instituto Superior Técnico - Universidade de Lisboa, Lisbon, Portugal
pedro.santos@tecnico.ulisboa.pt
[3] CEGOT – Universidade do Porto, Porto, Portugal
[4] Universidade do Porto, Porto, Portugal

Abstract. The Atlas of the Video Game Industry in Portugal published its second edition in 2020, with the main goal of mapping, characterizing, and analyzing the evolution of the video game industry on a national scale. This paper presents information on the current situation and recent trends (2016–2020) in the video game sector in Portugal (companies, employment, products, economic and financial situation, networks, and public support), as well as the main expectations regarding the development of this industry in the national context. Methodologically, the video game sector is characterized based on the collection and analysis of original data from a survey conducted with video game companies and independent creators, which develop activities in Portugal.

Keywords: Video Game Industry · Mapping · Innovation · Creative industries · Public policies · Portugal

1 Introduction

In the last few decades, the video game sector has witnessed extraordinary development worldwide. The global market has registered steady growth since 2016, generating revenues in the order of US$ 134.9 billion in 2018, and forecasts predict this growth will be maintained, at an average annual rate of 9.3%, reaching US$ 159.3 billion in 2020 and 174 billion in 2021 (Newzoo 2019; Newzoo 2020).

2020 has witnessed many global changes in the video game industry due to the novel Coronavirus (COVID-19) pandemic. Video games are playing a crucial role in the current context of exceptional measures adopted to respond to the pandemic. The lockdown measures and confinement rules across the world, complemented with recommendations to avoid large gatherings of people, have led to not only an increase in game use but also to consumers spending more time gaming than ever (Balhara et al. 2020; Ellis et al. 2020; Gabbiadini et al. 2020). This growing interest in gaming in this atypical environment means video games have come to play a major social role, not only as an easy in-house entertainment option but also as a way to promote social interaction by connecting people

© Springer Nature Switzerland AG 2022
I. Barbedo et al. (Eds.): VJ 2020, CCIS 1531, pp. 15–32, 2022.
https://doi.org/10.1007/978-3-030-95305-8_2

through a shared experience. This potential of video games as a social activity has been explored like never before over the last few months, especially by people who have come to regard traditional social media as very limited in their social connection experience. Indeed, new connectivity technologies have allowed video games to become much more immersive social networks.

Recent forecasts predict a worldwide increase of 135 million new video games players just in 2020, expressing an unprecedented level of engagement that will be responsible for huge market growth in the coming years, which is expected to exceed the global US$ 200 billion mark in 2023 (Newzoo 2020). Even though Europe has not spearheaded this industry, we find the same dynamics of steady growth in the video game industry, which generated US$ 21 billion in 2018 (ISFE 2019) and US$ 21.6 billion in 2019 (ISFE 2020). However, there are substantial methodological differences supporting the figures presented in both reports[1], which underscore the limitations of any attempt to perform a comparative analysis between different markets, as well as question the relevance and reliability of the data they gather, which is currently one of the main constraints to the study of the video game industry. Nevertheless, we have chosen to list here the figures that characterize this industry, taken from the main secondary sources (the main reports regarding the video game market) only for contextualizing purposes, as a reference for the primary data collected in this study, which will be presented and discussed in the following sections.

Despite the difficulty in accessing reliable data, it is clear that, in addition to its relevant economic weight, this creative activity incorporates multiple aspects making it a complex sector that has, furthermore, a strong impact on other activities. First, video games are considered an important engine of entertainment, creating synergies with other cultural and creative sectors, such as cinema, music and design. Second, it is a highly innovative industry that has contributed to the development of new techniques and approaches (for example, related to learning, simulation and engagement) that are currently applied in areas as diverse as health, education or fashion. Additionally, video games also incorporate a cultural dimension and relevant sociocultural impacts (Rykała 2020).

The economic growth prospects of this industry as well as its multidimensional dynamics are largely related to several trends, including digital distribution, multiplatform video games, the growing diversification of the player profile, and the redefinition of the creator-user relationship.

---

[1] The Newzoo report assesses the size of the global games market combining data from primary consumer research (an survey of 62,500 respondents between the ages of 10 and 50 or 65, depending on the country, that represent the online urban population from 30 key countries), with data from an opaque predictive games market model that intersects very distinctive contextual metrics (household income, GDP per capita, app stores data, primary consumer research, financial information reported by public agencies and leading game companies). In its turn, the ISFE report uses sales data just from the leading games companies and representative agencies of retail and digital markets (comprising physical and online games), complemented with data from players behaviors drawn from a very narrow and limited sample of the European reality (a survey to which 3000 internet users responded aged 6–64, from just 4 European countries: France, Germany, Spain and the UK).

Although the rise in interest in video games in Portugal is evident, it appears that a systematic analysis of the sector has yet to be performed at national level. The Atlas of the Video Game Industry in Portugal, first published in 2016 (Santos et al. 2016), has now launched its second edition in 2020 (Romeiro et al. 2020), thus seeking to contribute to filling this gap. Its main goal as a useful source of information is to broaden the analysis on the size and characteristics of the video game industry in Portugal, as well as recent trends in its development. This paper will systematize some of the most relevant observations of this latest edition, designed to support decision-making and action in the development of individual and collective strategies in the video game industry, geared at promoting this economic activity in Portugal. In comparison to the previous Atlas, the main changes are related with the territorial concentration of video game companies; companies tend to be fewer but larger (in number of employees) and a higher proportion of these companies have multi-location units; a drop in the number of companies dedicated exclusively to the development of video games; a higher preference for PC games development; and a significative increase in the total revenues of its main economic players combined with higher confidence regarding the future of the Portuguese video game sector.

2 Methodology

The Atlas of the Video Game Industry in Portugal 2020 aims to analyze this industry at a national scale and is particularly focused on development and publishing activities. This study collected primary data through a survey specifically designed to explore the experiences and personal opinions of people who are directly involved in the development of video games - companies and creators.

As mentioned previously, this is a follow-up study of the findings from the Atlas of the Video Game Industry in Portugal launched in 2016 (Santos et al. 2016). Based on the first edition, we have taken an evolutionary approach to this sector. It follows a previously established structure regarding the findings and how the survey was built: characterization of the enterprise/independent creator; characterization of the video games created and the development process; the creation, development, and evaluation of social networking among the main agents of this economic sector and, finally, the identification of the main problems and obstacles to the development of both video games and the sector itself within the country.

The survey was sent to all the contacts of the updated database of companies created in 2016, as well as to different intermediate agents (SPCV – Portuguese Society for Videogames Science, digital media, higher education institutions, research centers, and business incubators). The database has been continuously updated, whenever we received new information about the current state of the agents or the creation of new agents. The survey yielded responses from 43 agents (29 companies and 14 independent creators).

In this edition of the Atlas, there were several obstacles to the inventory of agents currently working in this sector, which hindered the maintenance and updating of the database, as well as contacts with possible respondents. In fact, there is a lack of an updated official database of agents in this sector, which suffers from a high mortality rate among companies, as well as a high mobility of workers and a general lack of information.

3 Survey Results and Analysis

3.1 Creative Destruction

Generally speaking, the origins of this sector in Portugal date back to the 1980s, the result of the passion and dedication of independent creators who were entirely self-taught, gaining and developing skills in the creation of video games. They even managed to sell some of them internationally.

The 2020 sample shows that there are two distinct phases, the first being a long extension of time until 2012 and the second within the last 7 years.

The first phase comprises a period of consolidation, in which entrepreneurship in the sector began. However, among the companies surveyed in 2020, very few were founded from this period (only 3), whereas, by 2016, the survey yielded 13 companies from this first phase. Their absence in the 2020 sample is because some of the companies from this initial phase did not participate in the survey, but also because some are no longer in business. The fact that some of these pioneering video game companies have closed, indicates the short longevity of these types of agents, or the existence of merger/acquisition processes in which some companies grow through the aggregation of smaller ones.

The second phase of the sector's evolution in Portugal reflects a more dynamic economic activity, with the average entry of 5 new agents per annum (companies and creators), while also witnessing the 'disappearance' of some companies from the 2016 sample. The ultimate closure of these companies may be the result of the sector's growing maturity, reflected in the appearance of larger companies, or simply a trait of this sector, whose teams are continually restructured according to the video game that is being created and the institutional framework that it presents.

3.2 Geographical Breakdown

In terms of the location pattern of the video game sector in Portugal, the main conclusion is the geographical trend of the 2016 survey is maintained, characterized by the sector's strong territorial concentration, which seems to have been reinforced in these last few years.

Looking back, if in 2016 the companies were located in 16 municipalities, of which 3 registered more than 3 companies, in 2020 the companies surveyed were located in only 14 municipalities where only two have more than 3 companies (Table 1).

Noteworthy is that Lisbon registers the largest increase, currently concentrating more than 30% of the total number of agents in the sector in Portugal. However, if we consider the Lisbon and Vale do Tejo NUTS[2], this proportion rises to half of the creators and more than 40% (previously 38%) of the companies. Thus, it has become Portugal's main hub in terms of concentration of companies, although it loses prominence in the concentration of creators (63% in 2016 dropped to 50% in 2020). This points to a trend for new companies to concentrate in terms of location, while creators tend to disperse (in favor of the North, Center and Algarve NUTS). It should also be noted that in Continental Portugal, the North NUTS also reinforced its attractiveness for new companies, concentrating in 2020

---

[2] Nomenclature of Territorial Statistical Units.

a total of 34.5% of companies (while in 2016 it totaled only 27%), accompanied by a significant decrease in the Center NUTS. Also noteworthy is the Autonomous Region of the Azores which, despite the small number of companies, started to contribute to the video game sector in Portugal from 2014 onward. Finally, neither the Algarve Region (Algarve) nor the Autonomous Region of Madeira are currently contributing to this business sector.

Table 1. Geographical breakdown, by municipality, of companies and creators in 2020.

	Companies (nº)
Lisboa	8
Porto	5
Angra do Heroísmo	2
Barcelos	2
Cascais	2
Vila Nova de Gaia	2
Aveiro	1
Coimbra	1
Covilhã	1
Esposende	1
Funchal	1
Loures	1
Odivelas	1
Torres Vedras	1

Source: Survey of companies and creators (February 2020)

To understand this geographical distribution pattern, we must analyze the main factors described by both companies and creators as the most important for their location (Table 2). Both agents highlighted proximity to other companies and creators that develop video games, which indicates the importance of networking and establishing partnerships for the development of this type of projects, where face-to-face interaction is valued, relevant for the promotion of innovation and the transmission of tacit knowledge.

The second most relevant factor is, in the case of creators, proximity to other complementary creative industries, associated to subcontracting networks of which these creators become a part. Also, proximity to where the sector's events are promoted can be related to opportunities to meet other agents and establish new collaborations. In turn, the companies identified proximity to higher education institutions as the second main factor.

Table 2. Appraisal of the proximity of companies and creators to different agents, in 2020.

	Companies (Ranking)	Creators (Ranking)
Proximity to other companies / creators that develop video games	1st	1st
Proximity to higher education institutions in areas related to video games	2nd	3rd
Proximity to places where events related to the sector take place regularly	3rd	2nd
Proximity to other (complementary) creative industries	3rd	2nd

Source: Survey of companies and creators (February 2020)

3.3   International Integration of Companies

Generally, most Portuguese companies in the sector are restricted to a single location and to the national territory (Fig. 1). Only 5 of the 29 companies surveyed (17%) show the size necessary to branch out inside Portugal. Portuguese companies with branches in other countries have also been detected, exclusively in Europe, in France (3 branches), Spain, the United Kingdom and the Netherlands (1 branch each).

This data can thus indicate the beginning of a new phase in the video game sector in Portugal. Following the development of the sector's entrepreneurship, nowadays the first steps towards video game companies with a greater complexity in the management of their production processes appear to be taking place. This entails the integration of different development units that, in some cases, are located in other countries, which can also be a way of exploring the potential for integration in international projects.

It is also worth mentioning that only 2 of the 29 companies surveyed (6.9%) are integrated in international economic groups, being themselves subsidiaries of foreign companies that have established a production unit in Portugal (Fig. 1).

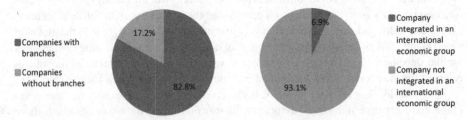

Fig. 1. Companies in 2020, according to the existence of branches and their integration in international economic groups. Source: Survey of companies and creators (February 2020).

3.4 Scope of Action of Companies / Creators in the Sector

Compared to the 2016 Survey, there was a decrease in the percentage of companies dedicated exclusively to the development of video games (from 68% to 52%), there being an opposite trend in the case of creators, whose percentage increased from 44% to 57%.

Companies that are not dedicated exclusively to the development of video games are mainly involved in programming activities. With slightly less expressiveness we find also consultancy and web design activities. In turn, the creators, in addition to programming (also the main activity), show a major involvement in multimedia illustration/animation activities (Fig. 2).

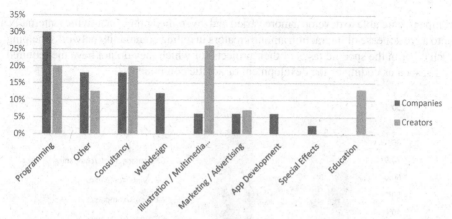

Fig. 2. Other activities, not related to video games, provided by companies and creators. Source: Survey of companies and creators (February 2020).

3.5 Subcontracting Relationships in the Video Game Development Process

With the exception of 1 company and 2 creators, all the other agents exclusively develop original games, continuing the tendency observed in the 2016 survey (Table 3).

More than 50% of companies collaborate under subcontracting in the development of video games led by other companies, whereas in 2016 this number only represented 1/5 of the companies, showing a greater level of integration by structuring deeper inter-business collaboration networks in the sector today. However, an inverse trend can be identified in the case of the creators (with a decrease from 69% to 64.3%), who remain the most dependent on the provision of services to third parties.

Furthermore, these agents are not only service providers, but they are also subcontracting promoters themselves (Fig. 3). Naturally due to their size, companies hire the most external services (44.8% of companies subcontract services to other agents, compared to 28.6% of creators). However, it is curious to note that it is the creators who work with a wider range of service providers (21.4% hire services from 3 or more providers, while only 17.2% of companies are in this situation). This could be due to the fact that

Table 3. Activities performed by companies and creators in 2020 (own video games vs. others' video games).

	Companies		Creators	
	No	%	No	%
Creation of original video games (authorship)	28	96.6	12	85.7
Collaboration on the development of video games (subcontracting per client)	16	55.2	9	64.3

Source: Survey of companies and creators (February 2020)

companies are able to develop a more varied and diversified range of activities internally, or to a greater ease of interaction among creators in online community networks, helping each other in the specific tasks of their projects for which they do not have the required skills, such as coding or the development of artistic components.

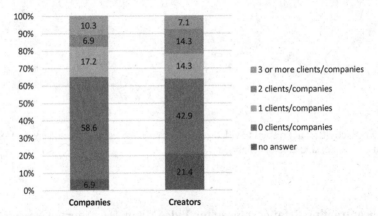

Fig. 3. Number of clients to which companies and creators provide services in the scope of video game development. Source: Survey of companies and creators (February 2020).

3.6 Employment

With regard to the volume of employment, it seems the video games sector has become more stable in recent years, showing furthermore a trend towards an increase in the number of workers of the existing companies. This trend denotes the sector's consolidation, albeit seemingly composed of fewer companies, but which tend to be larger in size suggesting a greater maturity in the sector.

The 29 companies surveyed generate an employment volume of 313 full-time workers, 29 part-time workers and 50 freelancers, corresponding to a total of 392 workers (Fig. 4), whereas in 2016, the sample of 38 companies totaled 375 workers. This suggests that Portuguese companies are expanding their size in terms of number of workers.

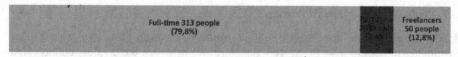

Full-time 313 people (79,8%)   Freelancers 50 people (12,8%)

Fig. 4. Persons employed in the companies involved in the development of video games in Portugal, according to their contractual relationship. Source: Survey of companies and creators (February 2020).

Generally speaking, it is estimated that the total volume of employment generated by companies in this sector in Portugal ranges between 986 and 1270 workers. In these calculations, the creators identified in the database of this project were not considered, in order to avoid double counting the workers (since some creators can be referred to by the companies as freelance workers).

It should also be noted that the average size of the companies increased from 10 to 14 workers, between the two surveys. This evolution reflects a relevant change because, in average terms, this business sector is no longer characterized as made up mainly of microenterprises, but rather of small companies.

The demand for workers with high academic qualifications has also been reinforced since the 2016 survey, when the human capital of about 45% of the companies was composed entirely of workers with university education, having risen to over 62% in 2020.

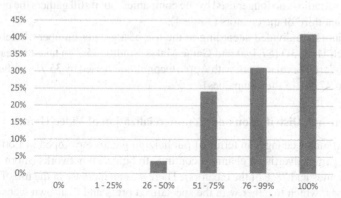

Fig. 5. Companies in 2020, according to their proportion of male workers. Source: Survey of companies and creators (February 2020).

It is also important to highlight that this is a sector where there is a significant over-representation of the male gender in the workforce (Fig. 5). In almost all the companies (96.6%), men are the large majority in the total number of workers. This characteristic may be related to a higher number of males in higher education associated with techno-logical areas, from which the human resources of this sector come. However, this feature deserves reflection regarding the manner in which it affects the future development of the sector in Portugal, as it will certainly have an impact on the genre of video games created and the target audiences.

3.7 Video Games Made in Portugal

From the 116 games developed by the companies surveyed, 38 (33%) proved to be profitable. In addition, 44 of the 183 games (24%) in which the creators collaborated made a profit.

In terms of the target platforms for which games are developed in Portugal, since 2016 there has been a decrease in web (online) and mobile games, and an increase in the development of games for consoles and PCs, which indicates that Portuguese companies are developing larger projects. More than 80% of the games are made for PC, and more than 50% of the games made by the companies are also intended for consoles.

It is also important to mention that most games produced in Portugal have a short development cycle (less than 18 months), with only 4 companies reporting they worked on games with longer development cycles.

3.8 Game Development Software

Since 2016, there is a clear preference regarding the use of certain tools used in game development in Portugal. Unity 3D is currently used by more than 85% of the Portuguese companies, as well as an exponential growth in the use of Unreal Engine (from 13.5% to 41.4%) and Android Studio (from 2.7% to 20.7%). In terms of programming languages, there is a predominance of C variants (C #, associated with Unity 3D and C + +, associated with Unreal Engine). HTML5 is also used by about a quarter of the companies. Game Maker Studio is no longer used by the companies, but it still gathers the preferences of more than a third of the creators (Table 4).

The creators are divided according to the use of a greater number of technologies, among which Unity3D (57.1%) and Game Maker Studio (35.7%) take the lead. A high percentage of creators also work with Apple technologies (used by 35.7% of the creators, compared to 27.6% of the companies).

3.9 Advertising, Distribution and Commercialization of Video Games

There are no major changes in terms of publicizing games developed in Portugal. The main video game advertising channels continue to be social networks (more than 82% of the companies and 78% of the creators). There was an increase in the use of YouTube for companies, which together with the specialized press and their own website is now used by more than 60%. Most companies (55%) also declare they use advertising, an increase of more than 10% compared to 2016, pointing to the companies' greater financial capacity.

When we analyze the data referring to distribution and sales channels, it is clear that there are more games being developed for PC and consoles by companies in Portugal (Fig. 6), and the use of Valve's Steam platform has risen (from 40% to almost 70% of the companies), to become the dominant distribution channel for this category. The Nintendo E-shop went from a negligible number in 2016 to 31% of the companies and 14% of the creators, which may be due to the success of Nintendo Switch, whose games are simpler to produce. There is also a reduction in mobile platforms, and the creators also show a significant increase in the use of aggregator websites (more than 60%), which have become their dominant distribution channel.

Table 4. Game Development Software used to design video games

Game Engine/ Coding Programs	Companies (%)	Creators (%)
Unity 3D	86.2	57.1
Unreal Engine	41.4	28.6
Visual Studio	34.5	28.6
HTML5	27.6	35.7
C + +	24.1	28.6
Android Studio	20.7	28.6
Xcode	17.2	35.7
Own Engine	6.9	14.3
Construct2	3.4	0.0
Godot	3.4	14.3
Marmalade	3.4	7.1
Rails	3.4	0.0
Cocos2D	0.0	7.1
Corona	0.0	7.1
Flash	0.0	7.1
Game Maker Studio	0.0	35.7
Stencyl	0.0	14.3
XNA	0.0	7.1

Source: Survey of companies and creators (February 2020)

3.10 Serious Games Developed in Portugal

Serious games represent the majority of the turnover volume for about 21% of the companies and creators, which corresponds to a slight increase compared to the data collected in 2016 (from only 11% turnover for companies and 16% for creators) (Fig. 32). The importance of serious games has risen slightly for companies (from 10% to 15% of the games produced in Portugal), with an increase in the number of companies involved in the development of serious games as well (22% in 2016 vs 38% in 2020).

An increase in the diversity of serious games produced in Portugal is also visible in this data. Among the companies that produce serious games, about 46% produce games for education/training (compared to 60% in 2016), with advertising games and games for the cultural sector now being produced by about 30% of the companies in this sub-sector.

3.11 Economic Situation and Support

3.12 Financing of Video Game Development Activities

In terms of sources of financing, there continues to be a very significant use of financing by means of equity among companies and creators in Portugal, with more than half of

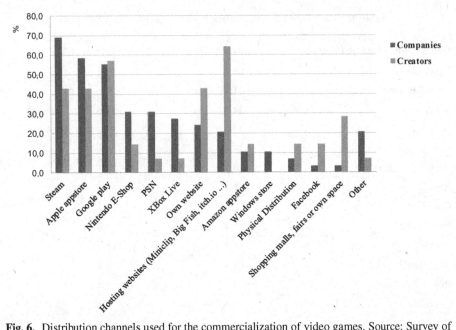

Fig. 6. Distribution channels used for the commercialization of video games. Source: Survey of companies and creators (February 2020).

the companies and 3/4 of the creators declaring this situation. However, compared to 2016, there are signs of evolution towards the use of external financing sources, with more recourse to business angels and venture capital.

Among the surveyed companies, 6 (20%) have obtained financing totally or partially through business angels or venture capital, divided equally between national and foreign capital. This situation contrasts positively with the situation in 2016, where only 2 companies reported this type of financing (Fig. 7).

While the companies refer to access to other sources of financing, in the case of the creators, all indicated the use of financing by means of equity, but those that are not financed exclusively in this way indicate funds from their publishers or a variety of sources.

Most companies do not even consider accessing credit to finance their activities. While the majority of the respondents has no formed opinion on access to these sources of finance, those with an opinion on the matter consider access to credit to be difficult or very difficult.

3.13   Sources of Economic Profitability

The most common source of revenue continues to be sales (indicated by 72% of the companies), with about half of the companies reporting also in-game sales (microtransactions). There is also a slight decrease in companies that declared advertising revenue (28%). The remaining categories have little expression, being mentioned by only 10% or less. The percentage of creators reporting revenue from sales increased by about 20%

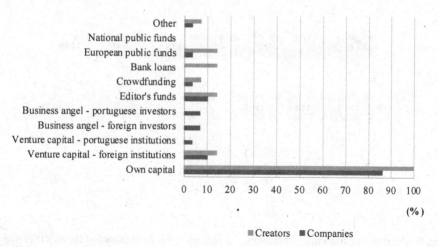

Fig. 7. Financing sources for companies and creators to develop video games. Source: Survey to Companies and Creators (February 2020).

compared to the previous survey (from approximately 38% in 2016 to 57% in 2020). In general, the creators indicated the same 3 sources (sales, microtransactions and advertising), and it is worth noting that 2 creators also declared they obtained revenues from the sale of physical products related to the video game.

3.14 Current Financial Situation

The data points to an increase in the revenues of the video game development sector in Portugal since 2016. Despite the fact that the largest company operating in this sector did not respond to the survey, given the importance of this component, we consulted official data for 2018 on its revenues and remuneration expenses. Thus, there are currently at least 4 companies in the sector with annual revenues in excess of 500,000 Euros, with the income of the largest of these exceeding 15 million Euros annually. There are also two companies with annual revenues between 250,000 and 500,000 Euros. In 2020, more than 40% of the companies declared having an average revenue of more than 50,000 Euros in the last 3 years, in contrast to the 20% that declared this amount in 2016. Furthermore, the number of companies that declared an income of up to 10,000 Euros decreased from 35% to 24% (Fig. 8).

The same trend appears when speaking of the creators. While in 2016 only 6.3% had declared income above 10,000 Euros annually, the percentage now rises to 28.6%. It should also be noted that about a quarter of the companies and a sixth of the creators refused to answer this question.

The data indicates a maturity and consolidation of the sector in Portugal, with fewer but more solid companies. If we try to estimate the total revenue of the video game development sector in Portugal, considering the average value of the response intervals and the conservative value of 750,000 Euros for the companies that responded in the highest interval, we obtain an estimate of about 4 million Euros per year for companies that actually responded. Considering that this number (22) will correspond to about one

Fig. 8. Revenue of companies and creators. Source: Survey of companies and creators (February 2020).

quarter of the companies operating in Portugal, we can point to a value of approximately 16 million Euros to which the largest company should be added, with a revenue of 15 million. Thus, our estimate for this sector's annual revenue should be about 31 million Euros, which more than doubles our estimate for 2016. The increase in revenue observed also seems to have caused a slight improvement in the financial situation of the companies (34.5% now indicate a favorable situation, against only 19% in 2016), and a significant improvement in the financial situation of the creators, of whom more than half declared balanced or favorable, against 25% in 2016. Once again, this data points to a significant degree of consolidation of the industry in Portugal since the last survey.

3.15 Networks in the Structuring of the Video Game Sector in Portugal

There is a tendency to favor the national scale in the case of interactions with higher education, research and development agents. Both companies and creators have more interactions with higher education in the field of video games or similar (universities and polytechnics), than with research and development centers.

At the business level, though, companies take greater advantage of the international scale than the creators. In the case of networks with higher education and research institutions, the national scale tends to be more exploited by creators, more than by companies, as they tend to favor networks of a more local scope.

It should also be noted that interactions with other complementary creative industries are those that are structured in a more balanced way at the territorial level, revealing, for both companies and creators, a more similar proportion of interactions between the three geographic levels considered: international, national and local.

3.16 Public Financial Support

In the case of companies, there is a decrease in the proportion of companies that have never benefited from any public support, from 94.8% to 82.8%. It is also important to note that only 5 companies and 3 creators reported having benefited from any public support (Fig. 9).

The range of public support used has broadened, revealing a general increase in all cases, going from 2.7% in 2016 to 3.4% for companies in 2020.

From the data, it is possible to see that the number of creators who have never benefited from public support has increased since the previous study (from 62.5% to 78.6%). They also show a preference for access to university support (7.1%, a fact that was not mentioned in the previous version) and access to support from the QREN (NSRF-National Strategic Reference Framework) (14.3%), replacing support from the MEDIA Mundus program (18.75% in the previous study).

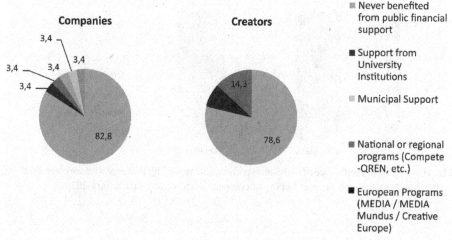

Fig. 9. Public support from which video game companies and creators have benefited. Source: Survey of companies and creators (February 2020).

4   Perspectives on the Future of the Video Game Sector in Portugal

4.1   Perceptions of the Economic and Financial Evolution of the Video Game Sector in Portugal

Both companies and creators showed an extremely positive attitude regarding their confidence in their continuity in the video game sector. This is a clear distinction from the answers obtained in the previous survey, with the largest increase being registered by the creators. Companies that responded they were very confident rose from 32.4% to 82.8% and, among the creators, the increase was from 28.1% to 92.9%. It can then be concluded that, although both perspectives have changed significantly, the creators are the most confident about the future of the sector in Portugal.

4.2 Perception of Agents About the Growth of the Video Game Sector in Portugal

This version of the survey reveals a more positive overview of companies and creators than in the previous one, with regard to the consolidation of the video game sector in their own region, with companies being the most confident in this regard.

A more positive overview can be concluded than in the previous version of the study, namely with regard to the significant rise of companies and creators that are very confident about the consolidation of the video game sector in Portugal (specially creators with 71.4% revealing high confidence, an opinion shared only by 55,2% of surveyed companies). Regarding those agents less confident (low or zero confidence), companies present a more negative view, at 44,8%, while the creators are less than 30% (Fig. 10).

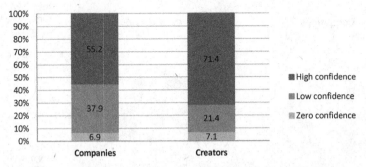

Fig. 10. Degree of confidence of companies and creators regarding Portugal's future consolidation in the video game sector. Source: Survey of companies and creators (February 2020).

5 Conclusion

In comparison to 2016, there are now fewer working companies, which can be explained by the dissolution of some companies, either because they were not viable or because they entered a merger/acquisition processes to gain size. In fact, there was a change in the composition of this economic sector, which was mainly made up of micro-companies in 2016 (less than 10 workers), but now has a majority of small companies (10 to 50 workers). Along with this trend, it should also be noted that the estimates made from the results of this survey indicate that the video game companies operating in Portugal in 2020 employ between 986 and 1270 workers and generate annual revenues of approximately 31 million Euros, a very prominent growth when comparing to the 6–12 million Euros generated by the 658 to 1204 total employees identified in the previous study (Santos et al., 2016). Thus, in Portugal there is a tendency to increase the companies' size in terms of number of employees and the volume of the companies' revenues, indicating that we are moving towards a consolidation of the sector.

Over the past 4 years, this sector has tended toward geographic concentration around the main urban-metropolitan areas in Portugal, which has reinforced troubling territorial asymmetries. Concentrating these activities which are more intensive in knowledge, innovation, technology and creativity severely underpins uneven regional development.

As for employment, it has evolved towards greater qualification and specialization, although Portugal faces difficulties in terms of retaining its most qualified professionals. This is mainly due to the small economic dimension of its projects, so measures to support the sector must include the structuring of transnational networks that promote the insertion of local producers in global value chains, namely through efforts to attract FDI in this sector of activity. Still in relation to employment, strong gender inequality is detected, which may restrict the present and future development of the sector in Portugal, as it will certainly mean limitations in terms of the genres and content of the video games created, as well as the target audiences they are intended for.

In the period from 2016–2020, this sector was responsible for the production of more than 70 video games, mostly for PC and mobile platforms, distributed in the international market, of which about 40% generated profit. These games have been developed despite the lack of external funding sources. In fact, this is one of the greatest obstacles to the growth of companies, and of the sector as a whole. Another major obstacle to the growth and development of the video game industry in Portugal is the lack of public strategies. There are no specific national public policies in Portugal to support the development of the sector, nor is there consistent regional or local support for these activities and promoters.

The results obtained in this study highlight the potential but also the main constraints to the development of this sector in Portugal. So, this study intends to contribute to more suitable public policies and actions to promote the sector's development and internationalization. The important role that public policies play in fostering the development of this activity is recognized internationally. We can mention, for example, Canada's positive experience with certain taxes exemptions to attract foreign investment or the creation of employment-friendly tax schemes (Barnes and Coe, 2011; Pilon and Tremblay 2013; Pottie-Sherman and Lynch 2019). In the case of Portugal, there are still no specific national public policies to support the development of the video game sector, or consistent regional/local support. However, the results of this study lead us to suggest that an ambitious qualitative leap is required, which is dependent on public measures that should prioritize three areas of action. First, an incentive policy should be implemented that reduces the tax burden on wages. Second, there should be support for financing this activity through measures to improve access to credit. Finally, mention should be made of various benefits and supports intended to bolster the country's attractiveness in terms of foreign business investment, such as simplifying administrative procedures or creating contact points with specific services that facilitate the reception of FDI in this sector of activity.

References

Balhara, Y.P.S., Kattula, D., Singh, S., Chukkali, S., Bhargava, R.: Impact of lockdown following COVID-19 on the gaming behavior of college students. Indian J. Public Health **64**, 172–176 (2020)

Barnes, T., Coe, N.: Vancouver as media cluster: the cases of video games and film/TV. In: Picard, R. (ed.) Karlsson, C, pp. 251–279. Edward Elgar Publishing, Media Clusters. Spatial Agglomeration and Content Capabilities. Cheltenham (2011)

Ellis, L., Lee, M., Ijaz, K., Smith, J., Braithwaite, J., Yin, K.: COVID-19 as 'Game changer': use and impact of augmented reality games on physical activity and mental well-being during the pandemic. J. Med. Internet Res. **2020**, 1–7 (2020)

Gabbiadini, A., Baldissarri, C., Durante, F., Valtorta, R., Rosa, M., Gallucci, M.: Together apart: the mitigating role of digital communication technologies on negative affect during the COVID-19 outbreak in Italy. Front. Psychol. **11**, 1–14 (2020)

ISFE: Key Facts 2018. Trends & Data. ISFE (2019). https://www.isfe.eu/wp-content/uploads/2019/08/ISFE-Key-Facts-Brochure-FINAL.pdf. Accessed July 2020

ISFE. Key Facts 2019. Trends & Data. ISFE (2020). https://www.isfe.eu/wp-content/uploads/2020/08/ISFE-final-1.pdf. Accessed July 2020

Newzoo: Newzoo global games market report 2019: Light version (2019). https://newzoo.com/insights/trend-reports/newzoo-global-games-market-report-2019-light-version/. Accessed July 2020

Newzoo: Newzoo global games market report 2020: Light version (2020). https://newzoo.com/insights/trend-reports/newzoo-global-games-market-report-2020-light-version/. Accessed Dec 2020

Pilon, S., Tremblay, D.: The geography of clusters: the geography of clusters: the case of the video games clusters in Montreal and in Los Angeles. Urban. Stud. Res. **2013**, 9 (2013)

Pottie-Sherman, Y., Lynch, N.: Gaming on the edge: mobile labour and global talent in Atlantic Canada's video game industry. Can. Geogr. **63**(3), 425–439 (2019)

Rykała, P.: The growth of the gaming industry in the context of creative industries. Reg. J. N. **20**, 124–136 (2020)

Santos, P., Romeiro, P., Nunes, F., Pinheiro, C.: Atlas do Setor dos Videojogos em Portugal (#1). SPCV and RAGE Project (2016)

Romeiro, P., Nunes, F., Santos, P., Pinto, C.: Atlas do Setor dos Videojogos em Portugal (#2). SPCV, Lisboa (2020)

Video Game Specialized Media in Basque Language

Maitane Junguitu Dronda(⊠)

Vitoria-Gasteiz, Spain
mjunguitu@gamerauntsia.eus

Abstract. This paper analyzes the situation of video game specialized media specific to Basque language. We focus not only on the available offerings in Basque language, but also on the informative demands of the video game consumers from the Basque Country. This research is set in the context of regional or minority languages in Europe and helps to draw the current situation of media in places that struggle to maintain their own identity and culture. First, we describe the specialized media in Spain. We explain the historical development of magazines and how video games reached the traditional media. Then, we take a general look at the specialized media in Basque language taking into account the sociolinguistic characteristics of the Basque society. As a case of study for video games, we analyze the blog of the video games Association Game Erauntsia. The next step is to study the demand of Basque speaking video game fans regarding their need to be informed. The data is interpreted after the survey conducted to members of the Game Erauntsia community. Considering the demands and the offer of specialized media, we bring up some conclusions that set new guidelines to fulfill the needs of the audience.

Keywords: Gaming culture · Specialized media · Basque

1 Introduction

Video games are an entertaining consumer product and part of a bigger ecosystem where media has an intermediary job between creators and consumers. Even if English is the common language used in the video game industry —big worldwide developers present their products in English with Nintendo as a singular exception in Japan—, there are many communities willing to enjoy the interactive and communicative experience in their minority mother tongues.

Such is the case of the Basque speaker community which is formed by less than one million speakers divided in two different European countries. In this research, we will describe the reality regarding the video game specialized media in the Basque speaking regions of Spain. We will look not only at the available media, but also at the wishes of the Basque video game fans. This research describes a media issue that helps to understand the linguistic situation of this European region where two different co-official languages cohabit.

M. Junguitu Dronda—Independent Researcher.

© Springer Nature Switzerland AG 2022
I. Barbedo et al. (Eds.): VJ 2020, CCIS 1531, pp. 33–45, 2022.
https://doi.org/10.1007/978-3-030-95305-8_3

2 Video Game Specialized Media in Spain

When it comes to video game specialized media in Spain, a decades long tradition of magazines has evolved into video game themed websites and the presence of video games on traditional media. All these aspects involving information about video games are studied in an appreciable number of academic research that focuses on this issue —especially within the undergraduate dissertations made by university Journalism students. This research is valuable to set a framework and go farther than the simple historical descriptions as they add specific analysis on the media.

Muriel and Crawford [22] point out how the media has evolved globally as video games cultural significance grew. They bring up that while the crisis of traditional print media did not kill video game-related magazines, a massive number of specialized websites appeared. They also compared the presence of video game information in traditional media with other cultural products like films, music or television shows. Even if TV hasn't traditionally been a place for video games, the evolution of the Internet and specifically YouTube —and after that Twitch— opened a place to develop video game related audiovisual content for large audiences, such as live streamings and pre-recorded gameplays or reviews.

Issac López-Redondo [19] in his Ph.D. dissertation reveals that the main purpose of specialized media is to guide the video game consumers in the wide market. Developers and distributors want to show their products and attract clients. At the same time, video game advertisements are the main income of specialized media. This creates, as López-Redondo says, a symbiotic relationship between distributors and media.

Carlos B. Torrado Silvente [29] observes that video game specialized media in Spain is divided in three different formats: printed media, printed media with an online version, and websites. He suggests that printed media didn't grow in the last decade and that branded publications, like the official Nintendo magazine, disappeared. Due to production costs, it is much cheaper to publish just online where there is also a lower degree of professionalization. Torrado Silvente enumerates seven specialized paper magazines: *HobbyConsolas*, *GTM*, *Micromania* and *Playmania* for information and *Retro Gamer España*, *Revista Manual* and *Game Report* for essay, interviews etc. market niche. In the last EGM report [9] —*Estudio general de medios* of Spain— *Playmania* appears as the 38th most read printed magazine with 155.000 readers per month. Some of these magazines were founded in the 80's. For example, *Micromanía* was created in 1985 and they are still selling, but others, for instance *Microhobby* (1984–1992), didn't last. Three of the mentioned magazines, *HobbyConsolas*, *Retro Gamer España* and *Playmania* —besides with the disappeared Nintendo magazine and *Micromania*, now property of BlueOcean Publishing— are owned by the German printing company Axel Springer.

Spanish video game specialized online media flourished during the 90's. Two of the main websites, *Meristation* and *Vandal* —both created in 1997—, are now part of bigger communication conglomerates that include traditional media. In the case of *Meristation*, it was bought by the big communication company PRISA. Nowadays, *Meristation* URL is within the URL of PRISA's sports newspaper *As*. The website *Vandal* associated in 2017 to the online newspaper *El Español*. There are several other websites that are part of big online media groups, such as Webedia, that owns *3DJuegos* (2005), *IGN España* (2012) — the Spanish site for the international IGN — and *Vidaextra* (2005).

Even if there are some specific video game related printings and websites, at the beginning, these contents appeared in information technology (IT) or computing related publications. That may explain what Silvia Martinez-Martinez [21] points out: vídeo games take the leap to traditional media in the «technology» section. The author is surprised that video games also make it to the «financial» section and how they are not significant in the «leisure» section. Martinez-Martinez remains that normally, traditional media in Spain doesn't have a «video game» section, but, when it comes to their websites, we may find specific channels or blogs that develop this topic. Of course, the exceptions are the cases previously mentioned, where websites were bought by communication companies.

Isaac López-Redondo researches deeply about the presence of video games in traditional and specialized media [19]. He concludes that printed Spanish newspapers don't publish many texts related to video games. He mentions two main reasons: the different audience profile of the newspaper and video game consumer and the year after year lesser physical space available in paper editions. Consequently, there is more information available on the Internet as there are no space boundaries. The Internet is also a place where technology fans get together. According to López-Redondo, this makes it the natural environment for video game consumers.

It is interesting that video games, and more specifically e-sports, found a place in the websites of traditional sports newspapers. The main Spanish sports newspaper *Marca* — according to EGM, the most read newspaper and the fourth most visited website in Spain— has included an e-sports section since 2017 that shows a menu divided in eight different trendy video games — *FIFA*, *Clash Royale*, *Fortnite*, etc. As we pointed out, the sports newspaper *As* — according to EGM the third most read newspaper and the seventh most visited website in Spain — added the specialized media *Meristation*.

When it comes to what kind of contents are the most usual, López-Redondo identifies video game information, releases and pre-releases, sales, billings, and company decisions. At the same time, he establishes the most common genres used by specialized journalism: editorial, news —including interviews—, articles, scoops, popularity and sales rankings, reviews, previews, downloadable games, retro, MMO, guides and tricks, readers' letters and bazar — mostly about merchandising but also texts about other topics like cinema —. Another interesting genre is the scoring ranking of video games, where the media evaluates the game following specific criteria like playability, graphics or novelties.

Of course, when it comes to online media, all this content can appear as a video or with a video complementing the text. Those audiovisual pieces can be any kind of content like trailers, interviews, reviews, tutorials or gameplays. Although there are some TV programs that traditional broadcasters scheduled uncertainly during last years — the last one a reality show called *Top Gamers Academy* (2020) broadcasted simultaneously in the TV channel Neox, Twitch and YouTube —, none of them had enough continuity to set a model. Besides that, there is still not any significant research about video games related TV shows in Spain.

López-Redondo explains that the way websites organize their publications is a heritage of paper magazines. He expounds that there are two main criteria to shape the information: first, according to the previously mentioned genres of the information and second, according to the platform of the video game — PC, PS4, Xbox One, Nintendo Switch, etc.

3   Basque Specialized Media: Writing for a Small Community

3.1   Peculiarities of Basque Speaker Regions

The Basque language involves sociolinguistic issues between geography and politics. This language is spoken in two different European countries: France and Spain. At the same time, Basque speaker regions are divided in two Autonomous Communities in Spain: the Basque Country and Navarre. In these three regions —the one in France, the Basque Country, and Navarre— the language has different levels of protection and officiality. That creates different social and political movements to protect, spread, and use the language in all aspects of culture, education, and life. This situation is not exclusive of Basque; there are many minority languages all over Europe demanding protection, such is the case of Breton in France or Irish in Ireland.

According to the survey of the Basque Culture Observatory — Euskal Kulturaren Behatokia — [18], only the 30% of the inhabitants of all the Basque speaking territory can speak and understand the language well or very well. It is a fact that a very small percentage of the Basque speakers are monolingual — only a few old people and kids that don't go to school yet —. Every Basque speaker is at least bilingual, as they know the official language of each of their countries, French, or Spanish.

To put it another way, Basque speakers can reach any media that is published in the main language of their country. All the media cited up until now is published in Spanish. This means that it is going to be understood by Basque speakers in the Basque regions of Spain. Despite that fact, we should question the situation of Basque specialized media —in general, not only video game-related— and the need of this in order to fulfill the informative necessities of Basque video game consumers.

3.2   About the Importance of Specialized Media

In the last few decades, access to cultural products in Basque language has been and it is still a concern for Basque society. That includes literature, music, cinema, media, and more recently, video games.

Arratibel and Garcia [3] state that the obligatory use of French and Spanish limited the usage of Basque language to the private sphere. The official languages became stronger in the public and prestigious sphere. This opinion is shared by Manterola Garate and Berasategi Sancho too [20]. Power-relationships that manage over society such as education and media — that helps to spread the prevailing tongue — are a bigger menace for minority languages than not knowing them.

Regarding media in Basque language, Azpillaga, Arana and Amezaga [4] explain that it appeared in the XIX century long after media in French and Spanish did. The first few attempts were in-between the Carlist Wars and the Basque magazines in North and South America. At the beginning of the XX century, several printed media appeared together with the ascent of Basque Nationalism. Some of them were about specific topics, such as religion, politics, culture and literature. These authors underlined the importance of the founding of the general information-magazine *Argia* (1919), that is still sold, and how the Spanish Civil War ended with almost all the Basque printed media. As Basque publications survived in France and America, it wasn't until the 50's when the concerns about Basque media increased in Spain. After dictator Franco died in the 70's the situation drastically changed and in the 80's Basque printed media consolidated.

Azpillaga, Arana and Amezaga believe that the first modern Basque newspaper, Euskaldunon Egunkaria (1990–2003), wasn't totally approved by regional institutions. These institutions didn't agree with the way the newspaper approached the movement in favor of the use of Basque language. In 2003, the newspaper was closed alleging links with terrorist organization ETA. At the end, the sentence of the trial denied any real connections of the newspaper to terrorism. In other words, the social, cultural and political prejudices closed the only daily newspaper in Basque language without any real reason.

As we see, the social and political situation, specifically in Spain, hasn't been an easy ground for any media in Basque language. However, during the last decades, a few weekly and monthly general and specialized magazines made it through. Azpillaga, Arana and Amezaga note *Argia*, *Herria* and *Aldaketa* as the most popular general information magazines and *Gaztezulo*, *Aizu!*, *HABE* and *Elhuyar* as the main specialized magazines. They mention several topics like academic, science, literature, learning of Basque language, religion, entertainment related and youth magazines.

Alkorta Zeberio and Zuberogoitia Espilla [1] define the diversity of Basque specialize media:

«There are quite a few magazines in the Basque language press that publish on specialized topics. However, each publication experiences a very different reality. In fact, while some are being released strong, others are on the verge of survival and death, in jeopardy. In terms of the characteristics of the magazines, they cannot be compared either in frequency, in the size and format of the newspapers, or in the way they address topics. We found very technical informational weekly magazines, as there are also lighter examples. »

Within the heterogeneity of Basque specialized media, the Basque Government [11] considered that even if they are important to normalize the language, the governmental protection of them is not a priority.

Alkorta Zeberio and Zuberogoitia Espilla [1] present a table with all the specialized media in Basque language. They determine the name, frequency, topic, and publisher of each magazine. They identify five main topics: science, medical and technology (1), human and social sciences (2), literature and culture (3), education, teaching and language (4), and leisure, travelling and consumerism (5). According to this list, we consider that video game specialized media should be in the last group, as the main purpose of it is to work as a guidance for consumers. It is interesting that the list does not include general information magazines that are addressed to specific audiences like young people as the magazine *Gaztezulo* does.

The Basque Government [12] collects the data about the most read magazines — general information and specialized—, not only in paper, but also with their websites traffic.

The list goes by *Argia, Aizu! Elhuyar, Hik Hasi, Ikastola, Gaztezulo, Administrazioa Euskaraz, Herria, Bertsolari, Axular, Jakin* and *HABE*.

It is noteworthy that the Basque Government [11] also points out that the future of specialized media —the one with a niche market—, is on the Internet. Paper versions of magazines do not feel important anymore. Hekimen [14], the association of Basque media, agrees about the importance of the Internet and underlines that Basque media increased their readers thanks to online publications. As recent examples of this reality, we can mention the new multimedia magazines for young people *Zut* and *Tapp*, both owned by different communication groups of the Basque Country.

3.3   Video Games Specialized Media in Basque Language

Besides the amateur blog *Pixelberri* [23] — founded in 2014 as a university student project — and the blog of the video game Association Game Erauntsia [13], there is not any specific media in Basque language about video games.

Without counting academic peer reviewed journals, there are a few specialized media about technology. The most well-known is *Elhuyar Aldizkaria* [10], published by the Elhuyar Foundation with online and paper versions. This focuses on traditional science and technology like engineering, medicine, chemistry, etc., and not in computing or consumerism aimed technology. Elhuyar Foundation works besides the public Basque Television, EITB, and they produce the TV show *Teknopolis* [28] in both Spanish and Basque. This TV show is more informational than the magazine and sometimes includes episodes about video games.

One of the radio stations of EITB, Euskadi Irratia, includes the radio-show *Sarean* [26], which again, speaks about technology in an informational way and often includes video games. This is a project of the PuntuEUS Foundation [24] to spread and protect Basque language, along the *.eus* domain on the Internet.

Between 2010 and 2013, EITB published an untitled blog [8] in Basque about technology — the Spanish version lasted until 2015 —. The texts were written by the journalists of *Teknoflash* — technology related short videos for the news — and the journalists of the *@bildua* radio-show of Euskadi Irratia. The description of the blog included a mention to video games and a specific tag in the menu.

When it comes to *Berria* [6], the only newspaper published daily in Basque, they don't usually publish news about video games. During the first ten months of 2020, they only published six pieces of news on their website. Five of them were in the «leisure» section and one in «finances».

The general information magazine *Argia* [2] sometimes publishes news about video games even if they don't have a category for them. For instance, in the culture section there are a lot of options like art, music, cinema, etc. but not video games.

Gaztezulo is the main paper magazine for young people. They publish texts about video games, social media, Internet trends, and other topics that concern the youth. However, the online version of *Gaztezulo* does not include tags to look for specific fields.

All the examples we mention are printed magazines, printed newspapers, or big media groups that include radio and TV have online versions. In addition to these, there is at least one example of a native digital media about technology: *Sustatu* [27]. This website was created in 2001 by the software developer company CodeSyntax. The goal of *Sustatu* is to share news about technology and any digital affair, most of them related to the Basque Country or Basque language, but also global and culture related. Video games is one of the topics they write about, but not the main one.

We also want to bring up the website *Kulturklik* [16] which is an online cultural agenda managed by the Basque Government. This website offers a professional section that aims to be an access point to information about any Basque creative industries, including video game developers. The website presents a specific section about video games including a company directory, financial guide, etc. This content is not informational.

Beyond the issue that there is not a video game specialized media in Basque language, there is a problem with terminology. The development of video games is not a particularly strong industry in any of the Basque speaking regions. According to the Basque Culture Observatory [17], the video games developers are the weakest of the creative industries in the Basque Autonomous Community. That means that there are only a few people creating or translating video games to Basque language. We believe there is a lack of terminology in Basque language that does not help to develop the video game industry.

Maria Teresa Cabré [7] explains that it is very important to create specific terminology to normalize a language. This is an issue that affects not only a certain technical field, but also all the speakers. The specific terminology allows experts to communicate between each other —and for extension to all people interested in a topic—, but also affects the modernization of the language and the ability to spread knowledge.

In addition, Jazinto Iturbe Barrenetxea, Martxel Ensunza Lekunberri, and Jose Ramon Etxebarria Bilbao [15] point out that when it comes to technological terminology, not only scientists and the Basque universities have responsibility over it. They claim that specialized media has an important role creating and normalizing words to allow communication between the scientific community and ordinary people.

The newspaper *Berria* made some achievements about Basque specific terminology in their stylebook [5]. They set vocabulary for sports, cinema, ecology, religion, festivals and even LGTBI, but not for video games.

4   Case Study: The Specialized Blog of Game Erauntsia Elkartea

Game Erauntsia Elkartea is the only association in the Basque speaker regions that works to spread video games in Basque language. It was founded in 2014 and besides organizing diverse in-person and online activities, they have created a blog where they post not only information about themselves, but also general information and news about video games. This blog is not a professional media but is the closest it exists to it in Basque language because it fulfills the purpose of guiding the consumption of video games. At this point, it is necessary to highlight that the author of the also amateur blog *Pixelberri* is a member of the Game Erauntsia Association.

Even if the main authors of the blog are members of the association, they also allow any registered user to post their texts. In that case, the post is reviewed by a member of the association. Regular authors are not professional journalists. The first professional communicator joined the association in early 2017 while the others are IT technicians and engineers. Anyhow, as they are the only significant content creators, their work can be considered specialized journalism. As Txema Ramirez de la Piscina [25] explains, their job has a social service value as they offer some information that no one else does with a deep knowledge in the topic. Together with that, they show concern about video game-related terminology in Basque language and they are constantly trying to find the proper words to use in their texts and along the community.

Since the blog was created in 2014 until the end of September 2020, they have published 650 pieces of news. Even though they have 24 different tags to categorize their texts, they don't offer yet a directory of them. Of course, the users can click on the tag and be addressed to the collection of posts that include that identification. The available tags can be separated in three main areas: video game related information — advise, articles, Basque video games, curiosities, discussion, festivals, guides, interviews, news, retro, reviews, sketch, tutorials and vlog —, information about the association and their activities — association, community, competition, contest, servers, translations and website — and pieces of news regarding other media — Aiaraldea, newspaper library and Ortzadar —.

The most used tags are related to information (Fig. 1). The most common one is «news» while almost half of the publications use it. It is followed by «articles», «reviews» and one tag related to the activities of the association, «community». The 25% of the publications are formed by the rest of the 19 tags, all of them with a lower percentage than 3,5%.

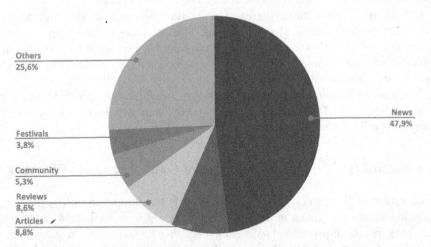

Fig. 1. The most used tags in the blog of the Association Game Erauntsia.

Over the years, the quantity of publications varied considerably (Fig. 2). Analysis took place from the first post on September 4, 2014 until September 30, 2020. It should be noted that during the 4 months of 2014, there were more posts than 2016, 2017, 2018, and 2019 combined. The blog had a peak of activity the first year after it was created and then the publication frequency went down. In 2020 the number of posts drastically increased and the first nine months concentrated 36,23% of the entire publications of the blog. This coincides with the moment where the association started working more professionally and hired two part time workers. 90,5% of the posts in 2020 were published by a member of the association that is a journalist but not one of the part time workers. The writer, who only posted two texts before 2020, just happened to be the author of the amateur blog *Pixelberri*. When it comes to writers that are not members of the association, in 2020 the percentage was less than 1%. That means that it is not common to have outsiders writing in the blog.

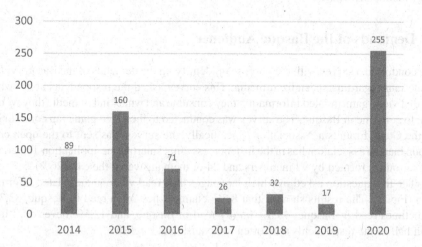

Fig. 2. Quantity of posts per year in the blog of the Association Game Erauntsia.

We attribute the descent of the publications after the first year to the lack of interest of the members of the association. As the excitement about the project decreased, the activity went down. We should not forget that it is a non-profitable association, what it means that they volunteer for writing. Only when they tried to professionalize their activities did they start working actively in the blog. It should not be forgotten that the contents under the tags «Aiaraldea» and «Ortzadar», only used between 2016 and 2018, were copies of texts that they published in professional media.

As an effort to professionalize the newsroom, the association decided to publish two texts every working day and exceptionally one during holidays and weekends. If we check the publications of 2020, we realize that some days they post the morning text while in the afternoon they share a video gameplay in another of the sections of the page. The website where it is established the blog offers many other sections related to video games and Basque, such as a gameplays made in Basque language, a list of Basque video games, reviews of the activities and competitions organized by the association, forums, and the terminology discussion.

All the publications have the specific elements of electronic communication. Besides the tags, the publications are also linked to the specific video game they speak about. That allows us to reach all the posts, gameplays and competitions that the website ever hosted about certain video games.

The readers that registered themselves as users of the webpage can publish comments in every piece of news. They can also evaluate the content of the text using a ranking of five stars. The website also offers the ability to share the content on Twitter and Facebook.

The blog agrees with the free software movement and all the contents are shared with the Creative Commons By and Share Alike licenses. As the purpose of the blog is to spread video games in Basque language, the creators want to allow anyone to use and copy their contents.

5   Demands of the Basque Audience

We conducted a survey with the purpose of identifying the demands of the Basque video game fans regarding specialized media. This survey asked the respondents about what kind of video game related information they consume and what kind of media they would like to consume in Basque. The survey was conducted to the video game fan community of the Game Erauntsia Association. Specifically, the survey was sent to the open chat group that the association has in the instant messaging smartphone application Telegram. This group is formed by 92 members and 24 of them answered the call (26%).

The first question asked in which languages they read video game related information (Fig. 3). The results showed that 8,3% claimed they often read in Basque, 33,3% sometimes read in Basque, 45,8% hardly read in Basque, and 12,5% never do. More than half of the respondents read often in Spanish and English.

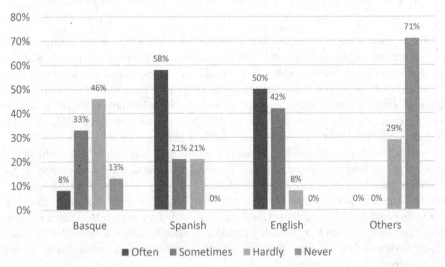

Fig. 3. Preferred language used by the respondents to read video game related information.

Regarding the amount of media in Basque about video games, 91,7% agree that there is not enough, and the rest do not care about it.

The main sources of information are the online version of specialized magazines (58,3% often read them) and the online specialized media (70,3% often read them). In fact, these two kinds are the most likeable to read if they were in Basque language (Fig. 4). The less read and less likely to be read in Basque are paper versions of newspapers and general-information paper magazines. About specialized magazines in paper, 54,1% never read it and there is not a need to exist in Basque language (50%).

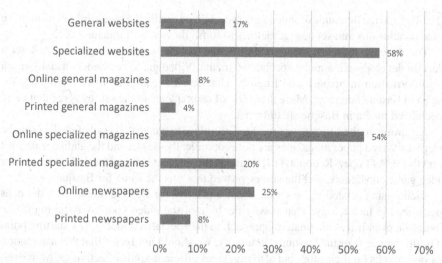

Fig. 4. Media in which the respondents prefer to read often video game specialized information in Basque.

The respondents often read texts (70,8%) and watch videos (66,6%). When it comes to podcasts, 62,5% barely or never consume it. Nevertheless, 75% would like to hear podcasts often or sometimes in Basque language.

We proposed nine different text genres in order to measure their popularity: news, articles, interview, review, preview, popularity lists, tricks, editorial, and players opinions. The four genres that reached at least 75% of likeable or very likable degree are news, articles, reviews, and previews. Reviews are the most popular genre and 87,5% agree that they like it much or very much. The least likeable content is editorial.

When it comes to video, gameplays (62,5%) and reviews (50%) are the categories that respondents like very much.

The 16,7% of the respondents don't visit the blog of the Game Erauntsia Association. Among the ones that visit the blog, only the 20,8% read it often.

The most popular genres of the blog are news and articles. The rest of the categories available in the survey — interviews, texts about the association, organization of contests, and gameplays — even if it is a small few, they have some respondents that claim they don't like it at all.

Finally, we asked about the contents of the texts. We offered five categories: video games in general, Basque video games, retro, worldwide festivals and presentations, and festivals and activities of the Basque Country. When asked about their preferred content, 60% of the respondents desired information about video games in general and Basque video games. With regard to festivals and activities, 85% preferred information on events in the Basque Country. This means that information specifically about Basque events was 35% more liked than festivals worldwide.

6 Conclusions

The offer and the demands of video game specialized media in Basque allows us to make some conclusions and set new guidelines to fulfill the needs of the audience.

The specific sociolinguistics reality of the Basque speaking regions didn't set a place to develop such a niche specialized media. Video game consumers usually reach this information in Spanish and English. That doesn't mean that there is no place for media in Basque language. More than 90% of respondents to the survey agree that more specialized media in Basque should exist.

According to the sources we presented, the place to create that kind of media is on the Internet. Printed paper magazines are not economically viable, and the audience doesn't want those. As López-Redondo [19] remarks, the Internet is the natural environment for video game consumers, and the survey proved that it is the same for Basque.

Video game related information is not a priority for Basque media even the ones specialized in technology. That is why the blog of the video game Association Game Erauntsia, even if it is an amateur approach to the specialized media, is a starting point to fulfill the needs of the Basque community. We should not forget that this association not only works on their blog, but also organizes different kinds of activities. Moreover, they are trying to set a specific terminology regarding video games in Basque language. We believe that creating that specific terminology will help to create video game specific non-amateur media.

There is a lot of work required to fulfill the needs of the Basque video game fans. It is also necessary to keep researching this issue, not only the situation of Basque language, but also the reality of other minority languages all over Europe and the world. In this paper, we offered a glimpse into the general situation regarding Basque media, and specifically about the blog of the Association Game Erauntsia. We think that a further and deeper analysis of all video game related information ever published in Basque, and particularly, of the publications and activities of the association, will help to open the way for professional video game-related journalism in Basque language.

References

1. Alkorta Zeberio, L., Zuberogoitia Espilla, A.: Masa-komunikaziotik informazioaren gizartera. Euskararen bideetan barrena. UEU, Udako Euskal Unibertsitatea, Bilbao (2009)
2. Argia Homepage. https://www.argia.eus/. Accessed 10 Jan 2020
3. Arratibel, N., García, I.: Euskareren egoeran oinarrituz. In: Arratibel, N., Azurmendi, M-J., García, I. (eds). Menpeko hizkuntzaren bizi-kemena. UEU, Udako euskal unibertsitatea, Bilbao, pp. 11–33 (2010)
4. Azpillaga, P., Arana, E., Amezaga, J.: Los medios de comunicación en euskera. Servicio editorial de UPV-EHU, Leioa (2010)

5. Berria Estilo Liburua. https://www.berria.eus/estiloliburua/. Accessed 10 Jan 2020
6. Berria Homepage. https://www.berria.eus/. Accessed 10 Jan 2020
7. Cabré, M.T.: Terminologia ala terminologiak? Hizkuntza-espezialitatea ala diziplinarteko alorra?. Uztaro: giza eta gizarte-zientzien aldizkaria **40**, 67–74 (2002)
8. EITB teknologia bloga. https://blogak.eitb.eus/teknologia/. Accessed 10 Jan 2020
9. EGM, Audiencia general de medios. http://reporting.aimc.es/. Accessed 10 Jan 2020
10. Elhuyar aldizkaria Homepage. https://aldizkaria.elhuyar.eus/. Accessed 10 Jan 2020
11. Eusko Jaurlaritza: Euskara hedabideetan Euskarazko hedabideak eta euskararen presentzia hedabideetan. Eusko Jaurlaritzako Argitalpen Zerbitzu Nagusia, Vitoria-Gasteiz (2008)
12. Eusko Jaurlaritza: Euskarazko hedabideak. Eusko Jaurlaritzako Argitalpen Zerbitzu Nagusia, Vitoria-Gasteiz (2015)
13. Game Erauntsia Blog. https://gamerauntsia.eus/bloga/. Accessed 10 Jan 2020
14. Hekimen, Euskal Hedabideen elkartea: Herri Ekimeneko Euskal Hedabideak, http://www.hekimen.eus/?smd_process_download=1&download_id=165. Accessed 10 Jan 2020
15. Iturbe Barrenetxea, J. Ensunza Lekunberri, M., Etxebarria Bilbao, J.R.: Zientzia eta teknikarako euskara. Zenbait hizkuntza-baliabide. UEU, Udako Euskal Unibertsitatea, Bilbao (2008)
16. Kulturklik Pro Homepage. https://www.kulturklik.euskadi.eus/profesionala/. Accessed 10 Jan 2020
17. Kulturaren Euskal Behatokia: Ikuspegiak. Sormen Industrien Estatistikako datuen irakurketa analitikoa 2017. Eusko Jaurlaritzaren Argitalpen Zerbitzu Nagusia, Vitoria-Gasteiz (2019)
18. Kulturaren Euskal Behatokia: Survey of Cultural Participation in the Basque Country. Eusko Jaurlaritzaren Argitalpen Zerbitzu Nagusia, Vitoria-Gasteiz (2019)
19. López-Redondo, I.: El tratamiento del videojuego: de la prensa generalista a las revistas especializadas. Análisis comparativo de las ediciones impresas y digitales de El País, El Mundo, Público y 20 Minutos. PhD dissertation, Universidad de Sevilla (2012)
20. Manterola Garate, I., Berasategi Sancho, N. Hizkuntza gutxituen erronkak. UEU, Udako Euskal Unibertsitatea, Bilbao (2011)
21. Martinez-Martinez, S.: La información sobre videojuegos como ámbito de especialización periodística. Comunicació. Revista de Recerca i d'Anàlisi **32**(2), 99–114 (2015)
22. Muriel, D., Crawford, G.: Video games and agency in contemporary society. Games Cult. **15**(2), 138–157 (2018). https://doi.org/10.1177/1555412017750448
23. Pixelberri Homepage. https://pixelberriblog.wordpress.com/. Accessed 10 Jan 2020
24. PuntuEUS Fundazioa Homepage. https://www.domeinuak.eus/eu/. Accessed 10 Jan 2020
25. Ramirez de la Piscina, T.: Kazetari l@na Euskal Herrian. UEU, Udako Euskal Unibertsitatea, Bilbao (1998)
26. Sarean Homepage. https://www.eitb.eus/eu/irratia/euskadi-irratia/programak/sarean/. Accessed 10 Jan 2020
27. Sustatu Homepage. https://sustatu.eus/. Accessed 10 Jan 2020
28. Teknopolis Homepage. https://www.eitb.eus/es/television/programas/teknopolis/. Accessed 10 Jan 2020
29. Torrado Silvente, C.B.: La evolución de la prensa especializada en videojuegos en España y su estado actual. Undergraduate dissertation, Universidad de Santiago de Compostela (2020)

It's Crunch Time: Burnout, Job Demands and Job Resources in Game Developers

Joana Mendes and Cristina Queirós(⊠) (iD)

Faculty of Psychology and Education Sciences, University of Porto, Porto, Portugal
{up201506965,cqueiros}@fpce.up.pt

Abstract. Although game development is a recent profession, many of its issues have been associated with the straining working conditions experienced by workers to keep themselves in the industry. This requires balancing job demands and job resources, and, in cases of extreme and prevalent job demands, it can elicit burnout as an occupational phenomenon. This study aims to identify burnout and job demand-resources levels among game developers, their relationship, and variation according to social individual/labour characteristics. An online questionnaire collected data from 193 game developers. Regarding burnout, results showed moderate levels of exhaustion and disengagement, while job demands revealed high levels of mental and concentration demands, moderate levels of time, emotional, material, and physical demands. For job resources, we found high levels of autonomy and moderate values of personal development, quality of personal relations, ethical, and social utility of work. Exhaustion is positively correlated with working hours per week and job demands, and negatively with job resources. The same happens with disengagement, except for mental and concentration demands. Time demands explained 27% of exhaustion, and personal development explained 14% of exhaustion and 51% of disengagement. Therefore, game developers face very demanding work conditions, alerting to the need to develop strategies for burnout prevention, and for the adequate manage of job demands using job resources, thus, promoting happier and healthier workplaces.

Keywords: Burnout · Job demand-resources · Game developers

1 Introduction

In May 2019, the World Health Organization [1] recognized burnout as an occupational phenomenon that affects several professions, due to job demands and the difficulties that workers experience while trying to adjust to them and using their job resources. The video game industry is roughly 50 years old, and it currently has a larger growth potential than many other creative industries, surpassing music and film [2]. Although game development is a recent profession, many of its issues have been associated with the straining working conditions experienced by workers to keep themselves in the industry. Throughout the years, multiple cases have been made public, denouncing the enormous monetary gain for the companies at the expense of their workers' health [3]. Yet, crunch

I. Barbedo et al. (Eds.): VJ 2020, CCIS 1531, pp. 46–58, 2022.
https://doi.org/10.1007/978-3-030-95305-8_4

remains a matter of concern to the industry, contributing to the experience of burnout and eventually leading its workers to leave their jobs and move to more sustainable jobs or even industries [3].

Therefore, it's necessary to understand how game developers deal with these issues and learn how they affect their health and their ability to work, in order to develop more effective strategies to diagnose, treat and ultimately prevent this problem in the future. Hence, this study aims to identify burnout, job demands and job resources levels among game developers, their relationship, and variation according to sociodemographic and labour characteristics.

1.1 Burnout

During the 60's, Freudenberger [4] and Maslach and Jackson [5] defined burnout as a syndrome of emotional exhaustion and depersonalisation that often affects people who work in human services, making the person feel dispirited about themselves and lacking job fulfilment. Emotional exhaustion is the major dimension of burnout, and it relates to being so emotionally overwhelmed and worn out by work, that it results in the depletion of the person's emotional and physical resources [6]. Depersonalisation refers to negative, cynical behaviours and emotions towards those whom one serves or cares for. This reaction might come across as insensitive and disinterested [5]. Finally, there is a feeling of reduced personal accomplishment, where the individual no longer perceives himself as capable of fulfilling the responsibilities of his job [6].

Exhaustion is usually the most apparent direct display of burnout. However, although necessary, it is not enough on its own to identify the presence of the phenomenon, because it fails to consider the relation that one has with their job. It leads to emotional and cognitive detachment from work, to deal with the overload. Depersonalisation then emerges to manage work demands, due to the constant feeling of exhaustion and discouragement, leading to a cynical behaviour towards the recipient of one's services [6].

Burnout has been strongly associated with negative consequences on one's job performance (e.g., absenteeism and turnover), lowering their productivity and effectiveness overtime, ultimately resulting in a reduction in their job and/or organisational commitment and satisfaction. This can lead to an increase in personal conflicts between work colleagues and disturbances in some related tasks. It also has an impact on one's health, especially mental health, and can lead to an increase in anxiety, depression, a lower self-esteem, as well to work-family conflict. Finally, burnout is viewed as a process that happens gradually overtime and it is not tied to a specific event or situation [4, 6–8].

1.2 Job Demand – Resources

The Job Demand – Resources (JD-R) model argues that there are particular risk factors associated with job-related stress in all activities [8, 9]. These risk factors can be divided in two main categories: job demands and job resources, which can vary according to the specific characteristics of one's occupation [9].

Job demands relate to all the aspects (e.g., physical, social, psychological or organisational) of work that involve the continuous use of cognitive and/or emotional effort and, therefore, have a certain degree of psychological and/or physical cost (e.g., workload, time pressures, and irregular working hours) [8–10]. The higher the level of activity, the greater the cost [8]. These demands are not automatically negative, since they only become job stressors when the workload surpasses the capacity of the individual to handle and recover from the effort [7, 11, 12]. This process drives the individual to use strategies to protect himself, but that too can have similar consequences over long periods of time [8, 9, 13].

Job resources refers to sources of motivation for one's job, whether by allowing to achieve work goals, reduce the cost of job demands or by stimulating the personal growth and development of the employee, therefore playing either an intrinsic or extrinsic motivational role in this process [8, 9]. In moments when job demands seem to be high, job resources can be particularly useful and influence work engagement and motivation. Furthermore, personal resources can also somewhat regulate this relationship and develop themselves through job resources [9].

1.3 Burnout and Job Demand – Resources

Since burnout is related with the work context, it is necessary to consider situational factors, such as specific tasks, as well as occupational and organisational characteristics, in its development. Factors such as workload, time pressure, role conflict (i.e., when conflicting demands of one's job have to be met), role ambiguity (i.e., there's insufficient information for one to be able to perform one's job well) and lack of social support from supervisors and co-workers have a moderate to high correlation with burnout [14]. Those that suffer from lack of feedback, autonomy, and have little opportunity to be part of the decision-making process are more likely to experience burnout [6].

Demerouti and colleagues [8], proposed the JD-R model, assuming burnout occurs when there is a clear discrepancy between the person's job demands and job resources. Thus, when job demands are immense and job resources are scarce resulting from unfavourable working conditions, it leads to a decrease in employees' motivation due to being in a state of exhaustion. This reasoning can be applied to any given type of occupation.

According to this model, burnout can, therefore, develop through two different processes. The first defends that extreme job demands at one's work can cause exhaustion. The second process argues that inadequacy or shortage of resources does not allow the employee to fulfil job demands properly, subsequently leading to a disinvestment in one's work [8]. Thus, it suggests that the symptoms related to burnout may develop under a specific combination of working conditions.

1.4 Game Developers

Since the 1970's with the development of Pong, the first commercially successful game [15], the game market has grown so much that in 2018 it produced over 131 billion dollars in revenue, and it is expected to reach over 300 billion in 2025 [16]. The Asia-Pacific region alone was said to reach 52% of the global game earnings, and the prediction is that it will continue to grow throughout the years, with China being the biggest single market in the world, grossing roughly 51 billion dollars by 2021 [17]. In 2018, Grand Theft Auto V, created by Rockstar Games in 2013, became the most financially successful media product of all time, raising more than six billion dollars in revenue and currently selling over 110 million copies worldwide [18, 19].

According McGuire and Jenkins [20], a *game developer* is someone who takes part in the production of a game, working on its mechanics (i.e., gameplay), content (e.g., art, music, storytelling) and technology (e.g., software), and can, therefore, integrate the art, design, programming, writing, or sound design teams. This could be done by only one person, a team of two, or up to hundreds. It is often the case that teams share certain responsibilities and, in some instances, it is also possible that one person can also be a part of two teams depending on the project and the size of the company. The authors emphasize that games are art as well as science, and as such a game developer must also be a multidisciplinary professional to meet the job requirements.

Regarding employment, according to the International Game Developers Association (IGDA) [21] 74% are employed, 15% work freelance and 11% are self-employed. In 2019 data showed the average tenure is only 2.2 years for employed individuals, this is due to being a project-based type of work, each game is therefore divided in three major stages requiring very different resources: pre-production; production; and post-production Hence, in addition to being a precarious type of project-based work, engaging in cycles of hiring, firing and reallocation depending of the stages of the projects, the worker is tasked to complete the project accordingly to the clients satisfaction by any means necessary [22].

In 2004 a disgruntled wife felt compelled to share with the world a blog post denouncing the working conditions at Electronic Arts (EA), revealing that its workers were facing constant crunch, being required to work up to 90 h per week. These long hours eventually started taking their toll on the employees, allowing them to be less effective while doing their jobs, deteriorating their health and, in many cases, leading them to even abandon their jobs [23]. Similar situations have been reported ever since.

Although most game developers love their work, there has been a growth in reports about long, uncompensated hours under extreme working conditions of "make it or break it". According to the 2019 IGDA survey most game developers work on average 40–44 h in regular weeks and 50–59 in periods of crunch. Crunch time is a term usually used in the game industry to refer to periods of extreme workload to ensure the release of the game in the time frame previously established. A lot of game developers tend to accept this kind of working conditions while still considering their job very positively and viewing crunch as a necessary and normalized condition to game development [21, 22, 24]. Additionally, unpaid, and unlimited overtime, poor work-life balance, musculoskeletal disorders, burnout, unsupportive work environment or lacking development opportunities are all issues that game developers often face in their line of work [25].

2   Method

To identify burnout and job demand-resources levels among game developers, their relationship and variation according to social individual and labour characteristics, a cross-sectional study was designed.

2.1 Participants

This study was conducted using a snowball sample of game developers, that is we relied on our participants to recruit other individuals from among their acquaintances to participate in this study. The total sample composed of 193 participants was obtained through the Portuguese and English version of the survey. Most of the participants identify themselves as male (78%), 20% as female and 2% as other, with ages ranging between 18 and 62 years old (M = 29.56, SD = 7.21). They were mainly Portuguese (46%), British (9%), American (8%), and 44% married or partnered. Their years of experience in the game industry vary between 0 and 35 years (M = 6.54, SD = 6.21), spending from 0 up to a 100 h a week working (M = 40.44, SD = 14.61) on their job. Regarding current employment status 64% were employed, 18% self-employed, 11% unemployed and 7% were freelancing. The majority of the participants were working in small companies with 10 or less people (37%), 37% were working at companies with more than 100 people, 21% in a company that employs between 10 and 50 people, and 5% in a company that employees between 51 and 100 people. In addition, their time in the current company ranged between one week and 15 years (M = 2.65, SD = 2.77).

2.2 Materials

The participants were asked to fill anonymously, either in the Portuguese or English version, a sociodemographic questionnaire inquiring about sex, age, civil status, country of origin, residency, country where they were working for, working situation, years of experience in the industry, dimension of the company they are working in, number of hours worked in a week, and whether they've ever experienced crunch along with the frequency and moments that it happened. This was followed by of the Oldenburg Burnout Inventory (OLBI) [26, 27], the Job Demand Scale [28] and the Job Resources Scale [29].

The OLBI has a total of sixteen items scored in a 5-points Likert scale (1 = strongly disagree and 5 = strongly agree) and divided into two dimensions: exhaustion (work overload along with a sentiment of physical, emotional, and cognitive depletion), and disengagement (negative and cynical behaviours and distancing towards one's job), both indicating that higher scores implies higher burnout level. The Job Demand Scale includes 28 items scored in a 4-point Likert scale (1 = almost never and 4 = almost always) split into five dimensions: time demands, mental and concentration demands, physical demands, emotional demands and lack of support, material demands and role ambiguity. The Job Resources Scale has a total of 31 items scored in a 6-point Likert scale (1 = strongly disagree and 6 = strongly agree) that divide into five dimensions: personal development, social utility of work, ethical, autonomy and quality of personal relations.

2.3 Procedure

The data was obtained through an online form, either in Portuguese or in English, shared within the online game development community. Participation was fully anonymous and voluntary. It was also solicited the collaboration of associations as well as newly formed unions such as Game Workers Unite UK and Game Makers of Finland in sharing the questionnaire with game developers. Data collection occurred between February of 2019 and June of 2020, taking a total of 16 months.

3 Results

A descriptive analysis sorted by dimensions reveals, in relation to burnout, moderate levels of both exhaustion and disengagement. It also shows high levels of mental and concentration demands and moderate levels of time, emotional, material, and physical demands. Regarding job resources the results reveal high levels of autonomy and moderate values of personal development, social utility of work, ethical, and quality of personal relations (Table 1).

Results also revealed that 85% of the participants report that they have already experienced crunch time at least at one point during their careers (Fig. 1). Of these, 80% reported no intention of leaving the industry in the foreseeable future, 10% reported that they had an intention of leaving now or soon and 10% were unsure of their stay in the industry (Fig. 2).

Table 1. Descriptive analysis of burnout, job demand and job resources' dimensions

Dimensions (range)	Minimum	Maximum	Mean	Standard Deviation
Exhaustion (1–5)	1,00	4,63	2,91	,768
Disengagement	1,00	4,50	2,51	,696
Time demands (1–4)	1,17	3,83	2,27	,607
Mental and concentration demands	1,71	4,00	3,09	,522
Lack of support, material demands and role ambiguity	1,17	3,50	1,98	,414
	1,00	3,50	1,62	,498
Physical demands	1,00	4,00	2,17	,610
Emotional demands				
Personal development (1–6)	1,40	6,00	4,89	,881
Social utility of work	1,00	6,00	4,26	,943
Ethical	1,00	6,00	4,76	1,305
Autonomy	1,25	6,00	5,02	,924
Quality of personal relations	2,00	6,00	4,87	,878

Comparative analysis considering sociodemographic revealed statistically significant differences (Table 2) according to sex, civil status, nationality, years of experience and the experience of crunch time. Thus, women in the industry tend to experience higher levels of emotional demands than men, and although not statistically significant women present higher levels of exhaustion and men have higher levels of disinvestment. Married or partnered individuals experience higher mental and concentration, and emotional demands than single, divorced, or widowed participants. Non-Portuguese individuals reported higher levels of mental and concentration, and emotional demands in comparison to Portuguese. Participants with more or equal to six years (senior) of

↘ No intention of leaving

▪ Intention of leaving now or soon

▪ Unsure of their stay

↘ Yes ▪ No

Fig. 1. Percentage of experience of crunch

Fig. 2. Intention of leaving the video game industry

experience report more time, and mental and concentration demands than those with less experience. Finally, those that have reported having experienced crunch time during their career experience higher levels of time, mental and concentration, and emotional demands and experience lower levels of ethical resources.

The correlation analysis (Table 3) revealed that age, years of experience in the industry, average of working hours per week and time working at the current company present a weak positive correlation with mental and concentration demands. In relation to number of workers at the company it presents a weak negative correlation with material demands, hence signifying that the bigger the company the less the individual will experience material demands, functioning as a protective factor in the experience of burnout. Concerning the average of working hours per week, it shows a weak positive correlation with exhaustion, time as well as physical demands, and presents a weak negative correlation with ethical. Weak positive correlations were found between the time working at the company and time and physical demands. In relation to burnout, the variable exhaustion correlated positively with job demands and negatively with job resources. The same happens with disengagement, correlating significantly with all job demands and resources variables, except for mental and concentration demands.

We executed a multiple regression analysis, utilizing the enter method, to understand the predictive value of sociodemographic and work variables as well as work demands and wok resources (Table 4). Thus, we were able to determine that work demands explain 32% and work resources explain 16% of exhaustion. In relation to disengagement, work demands explain only 12% while work resources explain 50% of this dimension.

Using a multiple regression with the stepwise method (Table 5) we analysed the contribution of specific variables, verifying that time demands are associated with higher levels of exhaustion, explaining a total of 27% of this dimension. Personal development is associated with lower levels of both exhaustion and disengagement, explain 14% and 51% respectively.

Table 2. Comparative analysis of job demands and resources according sociodemographic characteristics

	Female N = 39	Male N = 150	t student	p
Emotional demands	2,4974	2,0693	-4,054	,000***
	Married or partnered	Single, divorced or widowed	t student	p
Mental and concentration demands	3,2269	2,9894	3,278	,001**
Emotional demands	2,3765	2,0019	4,433	,000***
	Non-Portuguese N = 105	Portuguese N = 88	t student	p
Mental and concentration demands	3,2041	2,9627	− 3,240	,001**
Emotional demands	2,3181	1,9864	− 3,896	,000***
	Senior N = 80	Junior N = 113	t student	p
Time demands	2,3771	2,1947	− 2,075	,039*
Mental and concentration demands	3,2232	3,0025	− 2,953	,004**
	Crunch yes N = 163	Crunch no N = 30	t student	p
Time demands	2,3241	1,9778	2,930	,004**
Mental and concentration demands	3,1306	2,8952	2,296	,023*
Emotional demands	2,2160	1,9000	2,646	,009**
Ethical	4,6687	5,2667	− 3,341	,001**

*p ≤,050 **p ≤,010 ***p ≤,001

4 Discussion

Although we were able to find moderate levels of both exhaustion and depersonalization, these may not realistically represent the degree to which burnout is experienced in the industry. In fact, due to the healthy worker effect phenomenon, individuals who suffer from stronger levels of burnout may no longer be able or willing to participate in studies [30]. Moreover, workers affected early on in their careers by burnout are no longer in their jobs, suggesting that the respondents are the survivors, hence presenting lower levels of burnout than expected [6]. Finally, the moderate levels of job resources can function as a protective effect, mitigating the development of burnout [9].

The underrepresentation of women in the industry may help explain why they experience higher levels of emotional demands [22]. Additionally, the majority represent roles within art, project management and non-development roles (e.g., management, marketing, human resources) [31], which due to the specifications of the job might require more

Table 3. Pearson correlation between individual characteristics, burnout, job demands and job resources' dimensions

	Age	Experience in industry	Work hours per week	Experience current company	Number of workers current company	1	2	3	4	5	6	7	8	9	10	11
Exhaustion	-,033	-,020	,189*	,084	-,072											
Disengagement	-,080	-,032	,095	-,017	,031	,697**										
Time demands	,022	,068	,253**	,188*	-,054	,469**	,254**									
Mental and concentration demands	,199**	,148*	,211**	,241**	-,039	,303**	,046	,486**								
Material demands	-,021	-,060	-,096	-,016	-,187*	,322**	,236**	,175*	,236**							
Physical demands	,029	,063	,247**	,194*	-,114	,503**	,322**	,450**	,465**	,314**						
Emotional demands	,087	,049	,121	,079	,011	,282**	,185**	,405**	,510**	,322**	,427**					
Personal development	,009	-,036	-,042	,029	-,142	-,491**	-,729**	-,197**	,066	-,118	-,264**	-,148*				
Social utility of work	-,001	,024	-,124	,027	-,073	-,267**	-,439**	-,099	,054	-,125	-,122	-,088	,469**			
Ethical	-,073	-,051	-,186*	,013	-,135	-,414**	-,550**	-,282**	-,044	-,168*	-,359**	-,271**	,617**	,310**		
Autonomy	-,077	,022	-,049	,085	-,075	-,404**	-,539**	-,214**	-,011	-,107	-,257**	-,202**	,764**	,305**	,567**	
Quality of personal relations	,055	-,005	-,111	-,119	,095	-,291**	-,356**	-,106	-,055	-,225**	-,281*	-,150*	,358**	,369**	,371**	,274*

*p < 0.050 ** p < 0.010

Table 4. Multiple regression (enter method) for burnout's predictors

Dimensions	Predictors	R^2	R^2 change	F	p
Exhaustion	Sociodemographic variables	,026	,026	1,222	,304
	Work variables	,066	,039	1,371	,247
	Work demands	,384	,318	13,023	,000***
	Work resources	,541	,157	8,296	,000***
Disengagement	Sociodemographic variables	,030	,030	1,386	,250
	Work variables	,039	,009	,309	,872
	Work demands	,158	,119	3,554	,005**
	Work resources	,656	,498	34,982	,000***

*p ≤,050 **p ≤,010 ***p ≤,001

Table 5. Multiple regression (stepwise method) for burnout's predictors

Dimensions	Predictor		R^2	R^2 change	β	t	F	p
Exhaustion	Work demands	Time demands	,270	,270	,244	3,323	50,638	,001**
		Material demands	,329	,059	,269	3,948	12,056	,000***
		Physical demands	,366	,037	,191	2,928	7,814	,004**
	Work resources	Personal development	,502	,136	-,380	-6,048	36,576	,000***
Disengagement	Work demands	Physical demands	,093	,093	,090	1,609	14,104	,110
	Work resources	Personal development	,607	,514	-,634	-9,695	177,716	,000***
		Ethical	,629	,022	-,190	-2,805	7,870	,006**

*p ≤,050 **p ≤,010 ***p ≤,001

emotional demands. Results regarding the civil status may be related to a work-family conflict, allowing the individual to feel a higher level of emotional and mental demands while trying to balance both aspects of his life.

The fact that non-Portuguese nationals experience higher levels of mental and emotional demands might be related with both the competitiveness of the industry and labour market internationally. Therefore, non-Portuguese individuals have more contact with bigger companies with recognized brands and franchises, as such they participate in more noticeable projects with more responsibility, changes, and tighter deadlines.

Also, data shows that individuals with higher levels of experience in the industry encounter a higher degree of time and mental demands. This might be related to the underlying requirements of their position: doing more demanding tasks, needing a wider skillset, acquired responsibilities, coordinating, and supervising larger teams. Thus, their time is mostly spent overseeing the work of others and less on executing other important tasks. The experience of crunch shows that working conditions with extreme job demands can easily take toll on individuals. Additionally, the lower levels of ethical resources in those that have experienced crunch demonstrate a violation of the psychological contract and disrespect of equity and justice [6]. Furthermore, the fact that time demands explain 27% of exhaustion displays the risk that crunch presents to the appearance of burnout, while personal development functions as a protective factor to its occurrence, positively affecting one's work engagement [8, 9].

5   Conclusion

Despite being an exploratory and cross-sectional study, with voluntary participation, the results show that this professional group is often subjected to intense working conditions, with a high level of demands that they struggle to meet, leading to job turnover and health concerns, both physically and mentally. Fortunately, these concerns have started being addressed by the newly created unions, as well as news outlets for the past couple of years, making companies revise and change their policies. However, despite all these efforts, crunch still is prevalent issue.

This study can contribute to help identify the risk of burnout within the game industry, alerting for the need to prevent and even reduce this occupational phenomenon, such as EUROFOUND already suggested in 2018 [32]. Thus, intervention should be designed and adapted accordingly to the context, identifying job demands which have more impact on exhaustion, and work towards their reduction, while promoting job resources that increase workers' engagement, which leads to a reduction of both exhaustion and disengagement and could lead to an improved, healthier, safer, and happier workplace [8]. Future research should analyse whether there is a protective effect of personal resources, namely against crunch.

References

1. WHO: https://www.who.int/mental_health/evidence/burn-out/en/. Accessed 22 Aug 2020
2. Santos, P.A., Romeiro, P., Nunes, F., Hollins, P., Riestra, R.: A survey of the video game industry in Portugal. Revista de Ciências da Computação **12**, 1–24 (2017)
3. Macgregor, J.: https://www.pcgamer.com/the-pressure-to-constantly-update-games-ispush ing-the-industry-to-a-breaking-point/. Accessed 01 June 2019
4. Freudenberger, J.: Staff burn-out. J. Soc. Issues **30**(1), 159–165 (1974)
5. Maslach, C., Jackson, S.E.: The measurement of experienced burnout. J. Organ. Behav. **2**(2), 99–113 (1981)
6. Maslach, C., Schaufeli, W.B., Leiter, M.P.: Job burnout. Annu. Rev. Psychol. **52**(1), 397–422 (2001)

7. Demerouti, E., Bakker, A.B.: The job demands–resources model: challenges for future research. J. Indust. Psychol. **37**(2), 1–9 (2011)
8. Maslach, C., Leiter, M.P.: Understanding the burnout experience: recent research and its implications for psychiatry. World Psych. **15**, 103–111 (2016)
9. Demerouti, E., Bakker, A.B., Nachreiner, F., Schaufeli, W.B.: The job demands-resources model of burnout. J. Appl. Psychol. **86**(3), 499–512 (2001)
10. Schaufeli, W.B.: Applying the job demands-resources model: a 'how to' guide to measuring and tackling work engagement and burnout. Organ. Dyn. **46**, 120–132 (2017)
11. Colombo, V., Cifre, E.: The importance of recovery of work: a review of where, how and why. Papeles del Psicologo. **33**(2), 129–137 (2012)
12. Meijman, T.F., Mulder, G.: Handbook of Work and Organizational Psychology, 2nd edn. Erlbaum, Hove, UK (1998)
13. Hockey, G.R.J.: Attention: Selection, Awareness, and Control: A Tribute to Donald Broadbent. Oxford University Press, New York (1993)
14. Gauche, C., de Beer, L.T., Brink, L.: Exploring demands from the perspective of employees identified as being at risk of burnout. Int. J. Qual. Stud. Health Well-being **12**(1), 1361783 (2017). https://doi.org/10.1080/17482631.2017.1361783
15. Kent, S.L.: The Ultimate History of Video Games: From Pong to Pokémon and Beyond the Story Behind the Craze that Touched Our Lives and Changed the World. Three Rivers Press, New York (2001)
16. GlobalData. Video games - thematic research (2019)
17. Newzoo. https://cdn2.hubspot.net/hubfs/700740/Reports/Newzoo_2018_Global_Games_Market_Report_Light.pdf. Accessed 22 Aug 2020
18. UK Interactive Entertainment Association. https://ukie.org.uk/research. Accessed 22 Aug 2020
19. Valentine. https://www.gamesindustry.biz/articles/2019-05-13-grand-theft-auto-v-has-sold-110m-copies. Accessed 22 Aug 2020
20. McGuire, M., Jenkins, O.C.: Creating Games: Mechanics, Content and Technology. Taylor & Francis Group, Boca Raton (2008)
21. Weststar, J., Kwan, E., Kumar, S.: Developer satisfaction survey 2019.In: International Game Developers Association (2019)
22. Weststar, J.: Understanding video game developers as an occupational community. Inf. Commun. Soc. **18**(10), 1238–1252 (2015)
23. Ea-spouse. https://ea-spouse.livejournal.com/274.html. Accessed 22 Aug 2020
24. Edholm, H., Lidström, M., Steghöfer, J., Burden, H.: Crunch time: the reasons and effects of unpaid overtime in the game industry. In: 39th International Conference on Software Engineering, pp. 43–52 (2017)
25. Peticca-Harris, A., Weststar, J., McKenna, S.: The perils of project-based work: attempting resistance to extreme work practices in video game development. Organization **22**(4), 570–587 (2015)
26. Halbesleben, J.R.B., Demerouti, E.: The construct validity of an alternative measure of burnout: Investigating the English translation of the Oldenburg burnout inventory. Work Stress. **19**(3), 208–220 (2005)
27. Sinval, J., Queirós, C., Pasian, S., Marôco, J.: Transcultural adaptation of the Oldenburg burnout inventory (OLBI) for Brazil and Portugal. Front. Psychol. **10**, 1–28 (2019)
28. Morin, E.M.: Bilan de la recherche sur le sens du travail. Université de Montréal, Montréal (2000)
29. Gonçalves, S.P., Neves, J., Morin, E.: Looking for the Positive Side of Occupational Health at work. Universitat Jaume-I, Beniccàssim (2009)

30. Chowdhury, R., Shah, D., Payal, A.R.: Healthy worker effect phenomenon: revisited with emphasis on statistical methods – a review. Indian J. Occup. Environ. Med. **21**(1), 2 (2017). https://doi.org/10.4103/ijoem.IJOEM_53_16
31. Harvey, A., Fisher, S.: "Everyone can make games!" Feminist Media Studies (2014)
32. EUROFOUND. Burnout in the workplace: A review of data and policy responses in the EU. Publications Office of the European Union, Luxembourg (2018)

Game Based Learning in Science Fiction

Néstor Jaimen Lamas[✉]

Arsgames, Non Profit Organization, c/Sant Adrià 20, 08030 T, Barcelona, Spain
nestor.jaimen@arsgames.net

Abstract. In the following paper, three different science fiction scenarios in which pedagogy and video games meet will be analyzed, considering the aforementioned genre not only as entertainment, but also as an experimental and technoscientific laboratory. In these narratives, different problems will be analyzed with which to approach Game Based Learning in relation with psychometrics, behaviorism and non-directive pedagogies.

Keywords: Game Based Education · Pedagogy · Science Fiction · Video games

1 Introduction

In the following paper, three different science fiction scenarios in which pedagogy and video games meet will be analyzed. We will consider the aforementioned genre not only as entertainment, but also as an experimental and techno scientific lab. In order to do this, we use Gilbert Hottois' definition of technoscience:

> ...its actions and its products, result from the collaboration of a host of agents: research scientists from many disciplines, engineers and entrepreneurs, fundraisers and share-holders, lawyers and economists, commercial and marketing agents, etc. An essential aspect is that the subject of technoscience the actor, the motor and even the inventor – has become irreducibly plural: complex, interactive and inevitably conflictual (Hottois et al. 2018: 130).

That is, science fiction does not explain technology in a practical or neutral sense, but through its social, political and ideological implications.

From an epistemological point of view, according to the renowned science fiction scholar Darko Suvin, science fiction could also be considered "a literary genre whose necessary and sufficient conditions are the presence and interaction of estrangement and cognition" (Suvin 1979). From this other approach, its object is the psychological relationships between mankind and science. However, science fiction does not only deal with cognition. In many cases it produces knowledge itself and has even laid the foundations for modern sciences. C. Clarke is an example of this. In his book The City & The Stars, which came before Stephen Hawking's seminal theory (Clarke 2012), he outlines the concept of black holes; or the laws of robotics by I. Asimov, which constitute a milestone in the development of automatons (Anderson and Anderson 2011). Therefore, we can say that science fiction is a genre which lies between literature and

© Springer Nature Switzerland AG 2022
I. Barbedo et al. (Eds.): VJ 2020, CCIS 1531, pp. 59–71, 2022.
https://doi.org/10.1007/978-3-030-95305-8_5

science, as recognized by The Oxford Companion to English Literature: "not quite ordinary fiction, not quite science, yet partaking of both" (Birch and Drabble 2009: 892).

Even though science fiction does not comprise quantitative and systematic research, or any other model of scientific verification, it is constantly producing critical hypotheses that draw action routes for experimentation. This aspect attributes the genre futuristic traits. According to Kris Lovekin, science fiction is "the literary genre that describes how we got to the place we are going" (Lovekin 2000), or in George Slusser's, one of the biggest supporters of the genre, more poetic words "it is comparable to the wheel, the first and most important technological invention of the Western world. It gives meaning, reinvented over and over again, on a journey to a place no one has ever been". (cited in Lovekin 2000).

Without a doubt, science fiction goes beyond just mere entertainment. Not only does it constitute a place for technoscientific speculation, as we mentioned at the beginning, but it is an actor itself in the technoscientific plot because of its critical and scientific production. In such a manner, it isn't surprising that pedagogy is a field in which science fiction recreates itself, mainly as a science and technique that conditions other forms of knowledge. There is plenty of bibliography that analyze science fiction in education, as well as education in literature (Gough 1993; Michalsky 1979; Martin-Diaz et al. 1992). Likewise, video games, as a form of leisure and social interaction media, are a common topic among the genre, and its relationships have been studied from different points of view (Tringham 2014; Olson and Torrance 2009; Meskin and Robson 2012).

It is broadly accepted nowadays that video games can generate high motivation levels in kids, and so spark interest in topics which otherwise would be tedious for them (Oblinger 2004). Video games can also develop holistic knowledge (Van Ecke 2006) through mechanisms of trial and error, which are systems that we usually study separately. Although accepting video games in the educational field has gone a long way, much of the acknowledgment it receives barely mentions the practical aspect. We search for answers in science fiction because of its critical perspective.

It was not possible to find specific bibliography about the relationship between video games and education in science fiction, wherewith, the present analysis intends to be simply a revision of the literature that addresses this topic of current interest. It is not my intention to outline a theory on how these representations happen, nor am I sure it would be possible. Science Fiction is such a wide genre, that it can only be approached as a complex and heterogeneous corpus. However, the present study does intend to be a proposal on how to conduct an analysis such as this.

Being a literary examination, the hypothesis is that science fiction literature is an area which deserves being recognized and incorporated into current pedagogy and game based learning studies because of its speculative richness from a technoscience, and not merely utilitarian, viewpoint. Next, three literary works will be analyzed from a pedagogical approach: video games and psychometrics, video games and behaviorism, and video games and non-directive pedagogies. Be aware that for this examination, there will not be a differentiation between "hard" and "soft" science fiction, as it is usually done. On the contrary, it will be accepted that there is no clear boundary between science and fantasy, or technology and fiction, because of the speculative nature of this literary genre, and that it is precisely such ambiguity which generates the cognitive estrangement that characterizes it, according to Suvin, and provides the genre with the freedom needed to create scientific knowledge from hypothetical fiction. Along these lines we examine science fiction, for the purpose of this analysis, in the broadest possible sense and in all its artistic formats.

2   Video Games and Psychometrics: The Lawnmower Man

At the beginning of the 20th century, psychology was divided into two different trends. On one side, the German school of introspection, based on the subjectivity from a qualitative approach; on the other side, the Anglo-Saxon and American school, based on conduct from a quantitative approach (Pasquali 2017). Psychometrics derives from the second approach: it is the science that studies methods to measure and compare cognitive abilities. In the last few decades, this science has often been controversial (Carroll 1984; Conte 2005), nonetheless, during the 20th century and still these days, it had a major influence in pedagogy and particularly in psychopedagogical orientation by supplying apparently objective methods. In theory: "the incorporation of psychometric tests in the orientation process leads to the use of a scientific method which confirms what was observed, and the use of a measurement system supported by statistics as a way to ensure precision" (Alzina 1996: 97).

Moreover, psychometrics is the inescapable start in one of the fields which creates the highest expectations in cognitive sciences and biotechnology: cognitive enhancement. Firstly, without the possibility to measure an individual's cognitive abilities, it would not be possible to determine successfully its increase:

> An intervention that is aimed at correcting a specific pathology or defect of a cognitive subsystem may be characterized as therapeutic. An enhancement is an intervention that improves a subsystem in some way other than repairing something that is broken or remedying a specific dysfunction. In practice, the distinction between therapy and enhancement is often difficult to discern, and it could be argued that it lacks practical significance (Bostrom and Sandberg 2009).

Often, science fiction deals with both, psychometrics and cognitive improvement (Niccol 1997; Pfister 2014). In that regard, Flowers for Algernon, Daniel Keyes' only Keyes (2006), stands out as one of the most awarded and recognized novels of the genre. The plot tells the story of Charly, a young baker with a serious intellectual handicap, who undergoes an experimental operation to enhance his cognitive abilities. The successful treatment not only enhances Charly's intellectual abilities, but greatly exceeds the intellectual abilities of the people in his life, going from an IQ of 68 to 185. In other words, it's not only therapy. The gradual increase makes him gain language abilities and logical mathematical thinking first, and lastly, realize the abusive relationships he has with his family and alleged work friends, which leads him to an existential crisis.

Flowers for Algernon has been adapted numerous times, in movies (Ralph Nelson 1968), and even on The Simpsons (Anderson 2001). One of these classic interpretations is The Lawnmower (Leonard 1992), a B series movie which takes Keyes' plot but substitutes surgery for a video game and virtual reality therapy. The new premise implies that virtual reality, and specifically games, can overstimulate the brain to the point of increasing the patient's IQ in a very short time. In this version Charly is played as a gardener with mental retardation, victim of abusive relationships with his mother and alleged friends. As opposed to the novel, where the protagonist's suffering leads him to introspection, the lawnmower is not able to cope with reality after the therapy and uses his super intelligence to get revenge for all his misery. This puts the whole town on the ropes since the lawnmower, whose IQ exceeds any human being's, starts to use his intelligence to continue to increase his cognitive abilities and torment his fellow neighbors through technological control.

The theory the movie supports is no other than Jaron Lainer's, the technological pioneer who first coined the term "virtual reality" in the 80's. Actually, Dr. Lawrence Angelo, co-protagonist in the story, is his alter ego, as declared by the movie director (Carson and Springer 2012: 53):

> VR proselytizer and artist, Jaron Lanier, was fond of suggesting that the goal of VR is the construction of a personal "reality engine", an all purpose simulation device. This is far beyond what the technology can do, but developments far short of this goal may have effects on the amplification of human intelligence. The property of VR, alluded to by Lanier and embodied in this hypothesis, involves two aspects of intelligence augmentation: the attempt to simulate cognitive operations and the expanded experience of objectified semantic structures – exposure to predigested cultural understandings. As Jaron Lanier has observed, "Information is an alienated experience" (Biocca 1996).

Even though Lanier has recently recognized that virtual reality expectations have been modified (Tweedie and Steven 2017), numerous studies continue to confirm the beneficial effects of virtual reality in education (Radu 2012; Wickens 1992) and in psychotherapies (Coelho et al. 2012). In the same way, James R. Flynn in his famous study Are We Getting Smarter?: Rising IQ in the Twenty-First Century, concludes that in the first ten years of the 21st century there has been a general increase of the IQ index, which he calls the "Flynn effect". According to his conclusions, the increase in IQ is due to the greater number of problems to be solved in our modern life, which he claims are to a large extent caused by digital technologies and especially video games: "Video games, popular electronic games, and computer applications require enhanced problem solving in visual and symbolic contexts. If that is so, that kind of enhanced problem solving is necessary if we are fully to enjoy our leisure" (Flynn 2012: p.19).

In the last years, the relationship between video games and psychometrics has become closer: first, we see that children's video games have similar mechanisms to the problems that classic psychometric tests present, for example Raven´s Progressive Matrices; second, in the last few years, we have seen games that collect boys' and girls' data in order to allow parents and teachers to download psychometric analyses; lastly, video games are becoming more popular as a mental exercise in the classroom, and there are plenty of schools who own licenses for educational video games such as Minecraft or Kerbal Space Program (Fig. 1).

Even though these trends in education and game design have confirmed Lanier's theory, they take on a utilitarian approach which, unlike the outcomes suggested in

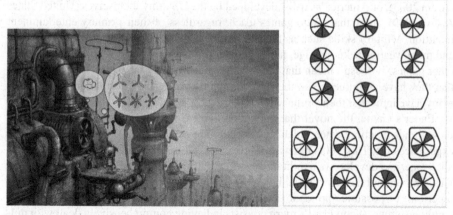

Fig. 1. Machinarium (Amanita Design (2009)) compared to Raven's progressive matrices (Raven et al. 2004)

Leonard's movie, take for granted that psychometric science is a beneficial technology in itself. On the contrary, from the hypothesis of this science fiction plot, measuring and enhancing psychological abilities can generate existential conflicts in an individual, as well as mental and emotional disorders that can originate from a radical, and not gradual, cognitive enhancement, and therefore should be supported with a critical reflection about the value and inclusion of other cognitive abilities. Without taking into consideration these matters, the advances which video games are already generating in the field of education can cause an opposite effect to what we expect: mental disorders and social marginalization, as the extreme case presented in The Lawnmower Man.

3 Video Games and Behaviorism: Ender's Game

Nowadays, learning through video games and computer software is a fact, not only in experimental schools, private and public, but also in well established programs such as the American army. Roger Smith, from the Human Resource Organization for Simulation, Training and Instrumentalization of the army of the USA, reported:

> The military has been using games for training, tactics analysis and mission preparation for centuries. Each generation has had to wrestle with the personal and public image of a game being used for something as serious as planning warfare (in which people's lives are at stake) [...]. For the first years of the 21st century, the industry faced a renewed vision of this matter with the expanded use of computer games taken directly from the entertainment industry (Smith 2010: p.1).

Since a great part of the army's learning process must, for security reasons, be simulated and can't be rehearsed until the situation demands it, video games are logically incredibly useful. Thanks to this, the army not only has managed to simulate extreme conditions, but has also become a way to educate millions of people, much before their enrollment. Games that are published on commercial platforms, like Call of Duty

(Arem 2003), or America's Army, developed by the US army themselves (United States Army. 2002), show that video games teach, regardless of their primary entertainment intention. Military skills such as tactical thinking, fine psychomotricity, concentration and mere weaponry knowledge, have become 'normal' baggage for enjoying these and other games. It doesn't mean that these video games can be labeled as educational, but that they have an influence on their users', mainly young kids, formation. This is why many have indicated their primary intention as propaganda.

Ender's Game, the novel that put Orson Scott Card (1991) on the map, predicted these trends in a time when video games could not generate such complex and realistic experiences yet. The plot is based on a historical war between humans and *insectors*, an alien race, and develops in a military space station with advanced educational technologies. Throughout the story the author shows his military knowledge and offers an ample repertoire of possible applications of game based learning that mold the behavior of children soldiers. Scott Card's merit consists in having comprehensively dealt with military psychology within an educational framework: motivation, emotion management, cognitive abilities, and psychological tests.

Broadly speaking, games and video games are applied in three different ways in Battle School where the protagonist character goes: 'battle', 'recreational game' and 'free game'. The first one is the center of all education in Battle School. It consists of a competitive sport which takes place in special zero gravity rooms. During training and competitions in these rooms, kids learn through theory, experiments, and mainly strategy. The second application, the 'recreational game', takes place in the arcade near the dining hall, where boys and girls measure their abilities and compete in various games. In theory, these games are purely for leisure, however, they are actually studied by the professors to find out which abilities stand out. Lastly, the 'free game' happens through an application installed in each of the tablets that are handed out to the students in the academy. This game reads the mind of the student and adapts to it. It presents challenges and roads in which they have to face particular situations or solve problems according to their psychological needs of the moment. The main goal of this type of game is to develop through positive reinforcement all of the student's potential without arriving at an emotional breaking point. It is supposed to be accompaniment and help, but it is also a psychometric test that teachers can use to get to know, examine and adapt their methods to the maturation process of the cadet's mind itself. Several scenes in the novel show how head school directors use these tablets openly as a form of surveillance, monitoring and manipulation of each soldier.

The 'battle' as well as the 'recreational games', are based on the same psychometric principles from The Lawnmower Man, as tools to measure and train the mind. Also 'free play' is an intentional psychometric test, but it is complemented with a different psychological science: behaviorism. According to the founder of this psychological school, John B. Watson: "Psychology, as the behaviorist views, is a purely objective experimental branch of natural science. Its theoretical goal is the prediction and control of behavior" (Watson 1913). Following this precept literally, 'free play' is a technique that allows tutors to know the behavior of his students and manipulate it through reinforcement, that is, with prizes that unconsciously reward the students for behaving the way their tutors expect them to. All of this in order to make war heroes from soldier kids.

The first person to use behaviorism in science fiction was, curiously, Burrhus Frederic Skinner, one of the most important theorists of the science of behavior. In one of his first works, Walden II, inspired by Henry David Thoreau's experiment, he builds a self-managed utopia based on behavior science and its techniques as a way to teach the inhabitants to be utterly happy. The protagonist of the story is one of the founders of this fictional community, doctor Frazier, who takes a group of students on a guided tour to show them around the place. It is he who guides the reader through Walden II and presents its good sides, although at some point he also mentions its risks. Frazier says: "When you have once grasped the principle of positive reinforcement, you can enjoy a sense of unlimited power. It's enough to satisfy the thirstiest of tyrants" (Skinner 1969: 248). This sentence shows clearly that behaviorism can be a powerful manipulation tool, as also shown in Ender's Game.

The power that Skinner is talking about is the same that the directors of the school use to deliberately manipulate Ender and his mates. Thus, what they call 'free play' in the book, is far from actually being free, it satisfies the most hierarchical of military structures. As a lot of modern research concludes, in the novel behaviorist reinforcement actually causes the opposite effect to freedom: emotional dependency and lack of initiative:

Grades, prizes and punishment, and authoritarianism in general, only eliminates the intrinsic motivation of the teaching-learning process itself and it in its place is substituted with extrinsic motivation that aims at receiving positive reinforcement (prizes, good grades, etc.) or avoiding negative reinforcement (punishment, bad grades, etc.) and at the same time reduces the responsibility of the students (Cabañes 2016).

Lastly, the 'free play' video console in Ender's Game is overwhelmingly similar to Skinner's Teaching Machine (Fig. 2), an automatic device that teaches children through behaviorism. Compared to today's educational game, strongly influenced by reinforcement techniques, this could be considered the first educational video game in history. And so, we see that what comes as simple fiction in Ender's Game, has its origins in a previous fiction that is actually science, produced by one of the most radical of behaviorists.

Nevertheless, the novel has a critical point of view towards this. Throughout the plot, young Ender comes to realize his superiors are leading him to a crisis with their psychological games, which later results in an anxiety meltdown. In the end, the protagonist becomes fully aware of the level of manipulation he has been subject to throughout his military career and that, even when he is the hero in the story, his life turns into an existentialist tragedy on the verge of suicide.

Fig. 2. Skinner's teaching machine (Clark-Wilson et al. 2017)

4   Video Games and Non-directive Pedagogies: The Veldt

Non directive-pedagogies, also known as progressive pedagogies, are those in which students make their own choices and take responsibility over the learning process. More than a pedagogical technique, it is a branch of education models that are based on shared libertarian values:

> In the face of authority, the ongoing maturation of freedom that each stage of development is capable of reaching. In the face of competitiveness, the development of individual abilities and personal effort that each being aims at reaching. In the face of conductism, liberation and acknowledgement of responsibility without guilt. In the face of punishment, reasoned dialogue. In the face of pre established programs, a rational and practical culture considering the maturation, interest and development of every individual. In the face of memory, understanding. In the face of stereotypes, creativity. In the face of subjugation, rebellion. (Luengo 1990:17-18).

More and more often, non-directive pedagogies are looking for a return to nature and matter, distancing themselves from technology (Cabañes and Rubio 2013). Their humanistic approach to childhood is often opposite to the trends in technological education. As we saw in the previous examples, virtual reality and video games constantly meet with psychometrics and behaviorism to create from education a more exact and quantifiable science, not always taking in consideration the students' needs, other than making them more intelligent and more well-behaved.

Nevertheless, in science fiction technological education is often seen as a detonator of these pedagogical models, as is so in The City And The Star (Clarke 2012), or The Fun They Had (Asimov and Conklin 1997). In Isaac Asimov's words, from his famous interview with Bill Moyers 1988:

Today, what people call learning is forced on you. Everyone is forced to learn the same thing on the same day at the same speed in class. But everyone is different. For some, class goes too fast, for some too slow, for some in the wrong direction. But give everyone a chance, in addition to school, to follow up their own bent from the start, to find out about whatever they're interested in by looking it up in their own homes, at their own speed, in their own time, and everyone will enjoy learning (Moyers 1988).

Following Asimov's train of thought, Information and Communication Technologies would have the same positive value to allow multiple educational paths according to the interest of every individual. In this way, someone that is more inclined to sports can give free rein to his interest, which necessarily takes him to other areas of interest, such as maths or physics. Most important of all, the learning process of an individual would respect his own pace and boost motivation.

Also The Veldt, by Ray Bradbury (Bradbury 2012), has a similar approach. First published in 1950 under the title of The World the Children Made (1950), this short story is especially interesting because it discusses a central matter for all nondirective pedagogies: the role of the tutors. A problem which arises when students are free. ¿How much are the tutors worth? Which should be their role? Or, how should they handle the students' learning process? According to Cabañes & Rubio:

The role of the teachers in traditional pedagogy set on an essentialist anthropo-logical concept, is based on the expert-pupil relationship. In this way, it stands by the idea that a school is the place where Knowledge is transmitted (Knowledge with a capital K, which means knowledge that is institutionalized, regulated and approved by a committee of experts who decide what is important, fundamental, and the basic knowledge that children should acquire during the mandatory school years before they reach adulthood and get a job) [...] Therefore, maintaining the role of teachers in free pedagogies is harmful because it reproduces the hierarchical relationships we keep trying to avoid (Cabañes and Rubio 2013: 73).

The Veldt is set in a completely automatized house. In this futuristic home, part of the children's education takes place in a virtual reality room which has the ability to read the user's mind and interpret with images, smells and sounds whatever it is he is imagining. The problem comes when Wendy and Peter, the two children using the room, repeatedly insists imagining an African savannah with two lions eating his most recent kill. Their obsession with this game alerts the parents, who are terrified and worried about the implications and the insubordination of their children. The situation escalates up to a psychological paranoid tension between the members of the family. In the middle of this conflict, the parents try to punish their children without the use of the virtual reality room, which produces an even more violent reaction.

To try to solve the problem, the parents agree to ask a psychologist specialized in analyzing the data collected by the system in the game. As in Ender's Game and The Lawnmower Man, we see again the concept of video games as a psychometric and data recovery method. However, Dr. Doolittle's answer is not the answer of a behaviorist, but of a psychotherapist concerned about his patients' personal relationships. On the contrary, he recommends the parents to spend more time with his children and not expect that the virtual reality room does his job as a family and educators, which is far from being an easy solution.

In conclusion, Bradbury offers a critique of technological solutionism which contraveys the expectations that video games produce as non-directive pedagogies in writers like Asimov or C. Clarke. Even thought Bradbury was also a defender of technological mediated education, he underlines the risks of non critical implementation, as if technologies where an instant solution.

Even though the story was written in 1950, in a time without video games, it is ahead of his time in regards to the relationship between virtual reality, games and violence and the increase of compulsive behavior, two problems that are widely studied these days (Delisi et al. 2012; Kuczmierczyk et al. 1987). It does so by showing game mostly as a means of symbolic construction. Maria Eugenia Villalobos points out in her article "The role of the teacher in the symbolic construction of children's play":

> Play is a favorable setting for development, since it allows the child to access the symbolic function [Piaget 1961]. When a child has access to the representational possibility, he is able to create alternative worlds to the real one, where transformation of his life experiences is allowed and new significance arises [...] There [during play] surges polysemy, transcending the literal world, static, rigid, when building significance of cultural worlds about previous semiotic processes of collective worlds. Hence the importance of the role of an adult that can offer children the thread that helps knit the senses (Villalobos 2009).

Henceforth, The Veldt is a warning to not leave a child to unattended play. It tells parents and educators that when they don't pay attention to their children's symbolic play, they become blind to their interpretations of the world, and might realize a bit too late that they show loneliness and resentment towards them.

5 Conclusions

In the last few years video games have been applied to education and game based learning, and have been shaped as a great psychometric and behavioral tool. Science fiction has been also speculating for over a century about the possibilities and often offers a critical vision that is not always taken into consideration in education practices.

The literary texts that were analyzed lay on the table how the benefits of video games in education settings can be diminished if the existentialist and semiotic dimension of the student is not acknowledged. In this way, uncritical manipulation of the behavior and cognitive training, without the proper guidance of an adult, and without taking into consideration the emotional dimensions of the student, are potentially detonators of emotional and psychopathic crises. This does not imply that video games are a useless educational tool. On the contrary, because it is such a powerful tool it requires an updated understanding of the roles of the teacher and tutor in order to make the most of it. Lastly, each case study brings to light that, in the research for a happy childhood and an education full of libertarian and human values, an unholistic vision of intelligence leads to planning counterproductive educational objectives.

Lastly the Veldt by Ray Bradbury gives us a different insight on non directive-pedagogies, and warns us not to rely on technologies as substitute tutors for the youngest. Even more, it addresses the constructivist role of the game process, making symbolic constructions, which is not often taken into consideration if education is reduced to intelligence and behavior. The results from these three analyses shows what we expected, that Science Fiction is a meaningful corpus where we can find critical and deep technoscience hypotheses. Regardless how old these books may feel, all three works analyzed showed that their primary intention wasn't just to fantasize with new fascinating technologies, but to outline crucial questions concerning education and its existentialist and psychological implications. Questions that, until this day, should be taken into consideration in education and video games developing process.

References

Alzina, R.B.: Orígenes y desarrollo de la orientación psicopedagógica. Narcea Ediciones (1996)

Amanita Design. Machinarium. Amanita Design (2009)

Anderson, M., Anderson, S.L.: Machine Ethics. Cambridge University Press, Cambridge (2011). https://doi.org/10.1017/CBO9780511978036

Anderson, M.B.: Homr. Gracie Films, 20th Century Fox Television (2001)

Arem, K.: Call off Duty. Activision, Infinity Ward (2003)

Asimov, I., Conklin, G.: 50 Short Science Fiction Tales. Simon and Schuster, New York (1997)

Biocca, F.: Chapter 3 Intelligence Augmentation: The Vision inside Virtual Reality. In: Cognitive Technology - In Search of a Humane Interface, pp. 59–75. Elsevier (1996). https://doi.org/10.1016/S0166-4115(96)80023-9

Birch, Dinah, and Margaret Drabble. The Oxford Companion to English Literature. OUP Oxford (2009)

Bostrom, N., Sandberg, A.: Cognitive enhancement: methods, ethics, regulatory challenges. Sci. Eng. Ethics 15(3), 311–341 (2009)

Bradbury, R.: The Illustrated Man. Perfection Learning (2012)

Cabañes, E., Rubio, M.: Gamestar(t): pedagogías libres en la intersección entre el arte, la tecnología y los videojuegos. Sello ArsGames, Madrid (2013)

Cabañes, E.: La Tecnología En Las Fronteras. Ph.D. thesis. Universidad Autónoma de Madrid (2016)

Card, O.S.: Ender's Game. Orbit (1991)

Carson, M., Springer, P.: Pioneers of Digital: Success Stories from Leaders in Advertising, Marketing, Search and Social Media. Kogan Page Publishers (2012)

Clark-Wilson, A.: The complex process of scaling the integration of technology enhanced learning in mainstream classrooms. In: Costagliola, G., Uhomoibhi, J., Zvacek, S., McLaren, B.M. (eds.) CSEDU 2016. CCIS, vol. 739, pp. 3–13. Springer, Cham (2017). https://doi.org/10.1007/978-3-319-63184-4_1

Carroll, J.B., Kohlberg, L., DeVries, R.: Psychometric and Piagetian intelligences: toward resolution of controversy. Intelligence 8(1), 67–91 (1984). (Carson, Mel & Springer, Paul (2012). Pioneers of Digital: Success Stories from Leaers in Advertising, Marketing, Search and Social Media. Kogan Page Publishers)

Clarke, A.C.: The City and the Stars. Rosetta Books, Maleny (2012)

Coelho, A., et al.: "Virtual Centre for the Rehabilitation of Road Accident Victims (VICERAVI) - IEEE Conference Publication. In: 7th Iberian Conference on Information Systems and Technologies, Madrid (2012). https://ieeexplore.ieee.org/abstract/document/6263233. Accessed 28 July 2020

Conte, J.M.: A review and critique of emotional intelligence measures. J. Organ. Behav. **26**(4), 433–440 (2005)

Delisi, M., Vaughn, M., Gentile, D.A., Anderson, A.C., Shook, J.J.: Violent video games, delinquency, and youth violence: new evidence. Youth. Viol. Juvenile. Justice. **11**(2), 1–9 (2012)

Van Ecke, R.: Digital game based LEARNING it's not just the digital natives who are restless. Educase **41**(2), 1–16 (2006)

Flynn, J.R.: Are We Getting Smarter?: Rising IQ in the Twenty-First Century. Cambridge University Press, Cambridge (2012). https://doi.org/10.1017/CBO9781139235679

Gough, N.: Environmental Education, Narrative Complexity and Postmodern Science/Fiction. Int. J. Sci. Educ. **15**(5), 607–625 (1993)

Hottois, G.: Technoscience: from the origin of the word to its current uses. In: Loeve, S., Guchet, X., Bensaude Vincent, B. (eds.) French Philosophy of Technology. PET, vol. 29, pp. 121–138. Springer, Cham (2018). https://doi.org/10.1007/978-3-319-89518-5_8

Keyes, D.: Flores para Algernon. Ediciones SM (2006)

Kuczmierczyk, A.R., Walley, P.B., Calhoun, K.S.: Relaxation training, in vivo exposure and response-prevention in the treatment of compulsive video-game playing. Scand. J. Behav. Ther. **16**(4), 185–190 (1987)

Leonard, B.: The Lawnmower Man. Allied Vision, Fuji Eight Company Ltd., Lane Pringle Productions (1992)

Luengo, M.J.: Desde nuestra escuela Paideia. Móstoles, Madrid. Madre Tierra, D.L (1990)

Lovekin, C.: Reading Ahead [Blog]. Fiat Lux (2000). https://web.archive.org/web/200703111 70147/http://www.fiatlux.ucr.edu/cgibin/display.cgi?Id=422

Martin-Diaz, M.J., Pizarro, A., Bacas, P., Garcia, J.P., Perera, F.: Science fiction comes into the classroom: maelstrom II. Phys. Educ. **27**(1), 18–23 (1992)

Meskin, A., Robson, J.: Fiction and fictional worlds in videogames. In: Sageng, J.R., Fossheim, H., Mandt Larsen, T., (eds.)The Philosophy of Computer Games, Philosophy of Engineering and Technology, , pp. 201–217. Springer Netherlands, Dordrecht (2012)

Michalsky, M.W.: Manipulating our futures: the role of science fiction in education. Clear. House: J. Educ. Strat. Issues Ideas **52**(6), 246–249 (1979)

Moyers, B.: World of Ideas. Public Affairs TV, USA (1988)

Nelson, R.: Charly. Selmur Productions, Robertson and Associates, ABC Pictures(1968)

Niccol, A.: Gattaca. Columbia Pictures, Jersey Films (1997)

Oblinger, D.G.: The next generation of educational engagement. J. Interact. Media Educ. **2004**(1), 10 (2004). https://doi.org/10.5334/2004-8-oblinger

Olson, D.R., Torrance, N.: The Cambridge Handbook of Literacy. Cambridge University Press, Cambridge (2009)

Pasquali, L.: Psicometria: Teoria dos testes na psicologia e na educação. Editora Vozes Limitada (2017)

Raven, J., Raven, J.C., & Court, J.H. (2004) Manual for Raven's Progressive Matrices and Vocabulary Scales. San Antonio, TX: Harcourt Assessment

Radu, I.: Why should my students use ar? a comparative review of the educational impacts of augmented-reality ISMAR 2012. In: 11th IEEE International Symposium on Mixed and Augmented Reality 2012, Science and Technology Papers, Atlanta, GA IEEE USA, pp. 313–314 (2012)

Impacts of Augmented-Reality. In: 2012 IEEE International Symposium on Mixed and Augmented Reality (ISMAR), pp. 313–14. IEEE, Atlanta, GA, USA (2012)

Skinner, B.F.: Walden dos. Argentina: Editorial Fontanella (1985)

Smith, R.:. The long history of gaming in military training. Orlando (2010)

Suvin, D.: Metamorphoses of Science Fiction: On the Poetics and History of a Literary Genre. Yale University Press, New Haven (1979)

Tringham, N.R.: Science Fiction Video Games. CRC Press, Boca Raton (2014)

Tweedie, Zoë Bernard, Steven (2017). "The Father of Virtual Reality Sounds off on the Changing Culture of Silicon Valley, the Impending #MeToo Backlash, and Why He Left Google for Microsoft." Business Insider. Retrieved June 17, 2020 (https://www.businessinsider.com/jaron-lanier-). Interview-on-silicon-valley-culture-metoobacklash-ai-and-the-future-2017–12

United States Army (2002). America´s Army. United States Army

Villalobos, M.E.: El rol del maestro frente a la construcción del juego simbólico en los niños. Diversitas 5(2), 269 (2009). https://doi.org/10.15332/s1794-9998.2009.0002.05

Pfister, W.: Transcendence. Alcon Entertainment, DMG Entertainment, Straight Up Films (2014)

Watson, J.B.: Psychology as the behaviorist views it. Psychol. Rev. 20(2), 158–177 (1913). https://doi.org/10.1037/h0074428

Wickens, C.D.: Virtual Reality and Education. In: Proceedings of 1992 IEEE International Conference on Systems, Man, and Cybernetics. Chicago, IL, pp. 842–847. IEEE, USA (1992)

Supporting the Construction of Game Narratives Using a Toolkit to Game Design

Pedro Beça[✉] [iD], Cláudia Ortet[iD], Mónica Aresta[iD], Rita Santos[iD], Ana Veloso[iD], and Sofia Ribeiro[iD]

Department of Communication and Art, University of Aveiro, Campus Universitário Santiago, 3810-193, Aveiro, Portugal

```
{pedrobeca,claudiaortet,m.aresta,Rita.santos,aiv,
                saribeiro}@ua.pt
```

Abstract. Students are being more often challenged not only to play but also to create games when there is increasing evidence of the impact, in terms of learning, of students' involvement in creating their own games centred on educational content. Nevertheless, the game making process has certain specificities that are not usually recognized by the public but are relevant to create good games. Taking this into consideration, the Gamers4Nature project developed a Toolkit to Game Design to support users, with and without previous experience, during a game creation process. This paper focus on the analysis of undergraduate students' engagement using the Toolkit through the creation of game narratives focused on environmental preservation. A total of 46 undergraduate students from a Social Sciences (non-ICT course) participated in 2-h game narrative design sessions, using the Toolkit's resources to develop their game's narrative. As a result, 14 game narratives were created. Participants considered the Toolkit easy to use, not having preponderant usability issues. Although additional tests are still needed, namely with larger and diversified groups, preliminary results indicate that the Toolkit is a resource capable of assisting users with no previous experience during the game design process, namely in the writing of game's narratives.

Keywords: Toolkit · Game Design · Narratives · Digital games · Environmental awareness

1 Introduction

Games have been part of human life since early times [1]. Present from childhood to most of adult life, in recreational activities and in more structured contexts, games are being played and used in different contexts such as education, industry, tourism and marketing [2–4].

In the educational field, games are being used to develop problem-solving competences, to provide contextualized experience and to promote collaboration between game players [5]. In game-based learning – *i.e.* learning through games – stories and narratives are seen as mechanisms of human learning and construction of reality [6] and a pathway to a new and effective learning approach to education [7–9]. Still in the field

© Springer Nature Switzerland AG 2022
I. Barbedo et al. (Eds.): VJ 2020, CCIS 1531, pp. 72–83, 2022.
https://doi.org/10.1007/978-3-030-95305-8_6

of games and education, it is important to remember that learners can be not only digital game consumers, but also game producers being challenged to create their own games for learning [10, 11].

It is widely accepted that the creation and development of games often requires individuals and teams from several disciplines, able to work together along the process of design a game. While the integration of individuals with different backgrounds is seen as a strength, it is also stressed that the lack of background and skills in the construction of games and game narratives may affect the game making process [12–15].

Starting from this premise, the Gamers4Nature project developed a Toolkit to Game Design, to be used by young users with and without experience in game design, to create games addressing ecological themes. The Gamers4Nature Toolkit includes a set of tools designed to support young users in the creation of their own games and to foster positive behaviour changes towards environment preservation. The environmental awareness theme was chosen due to the growing impact of climate change, biodiversity loss and pollution and other nature-related problems, and supported by the belief that an effort must be made to promote environmental awareness and knowledge amongst younger audiences.

The Gamers4Nature Toolkit to Game Design was used by undergraduate students with no experience in developing games along several game design sessions with the aim of create game narratives. This paper describes those sessions and its main outputs, and it is organized as follows: Sect. 2 introduces a literature review focused on toolkits developed to support game design and game narratives; Sect. 3 presents the study's methodological approach; Sect. 4 describes the created games' narratives and discusses the main results of the study; and in Sect. 5 final considerations and future work are presented.

2 Literature Review

2.1 Digital Games and Learning

Whether in leisure activities or in more structured contexts, games and playing have been part of human nature since ancient times [1], playing an important role in the development of intellectual, physical and social abilities, as in meeting individual's needs and preferences [16].

Even though digital games are often associated to negative behaviours such as aggressiveness, social isolation and addictiveness [17–19], research on its use also demonstrated positive impacts on learning, motivation, knowledge acquisition, skills development and behaviour change, either through the use of gamification strategies or by developing games centred on educational subjects [20–23]. Moreover, Digital games' learning values can be transferred to other learning scenarios (*e.g.* schools, universities and workplaces), and are all solidly endorsed by investigation in cognitive sciences [10].

In recent years, a complementary approach to digital games and education, focused on the benefits of engaging students in the creation of their own games has emerged [24–27]. Creating digital games was found to be highly engaging, pleasurable and gratifying by younger audiences [23, 28], with research pointing out that giving learners the possibility to create games on subjects related to the learning curriculum can be associated with an increased interest in the subject that is being addressed and a better understanding of the value of what is learned [15]; the acquisition of scientific concepts [29]; and the development of digital literacy throughout the design process [29, 30].

2.2 Toolkits to Support Narratives' Construction and Game Design

Toolkits, due to its problem-solving features and its support materials and resources, are nowadays seen as powerful learning and teaching tools, allowing faster prototyping, supporting creative design and assisting in the production of interactive artefacts [31, 31]. According to Oulasvirta and Hornbaek [32], a toolkit is often categorized into constructive research, and defined as the creation of comprehension about the construction of an exploitable artefact for some intent in HCI.

Toolkits are often developed and used in the field of Human-Computer Interaction (HCI), where they are used to support and influence the design and implementation of interactive systems [33]. In what concerns toolkits for game development, however, the focus is often placed on game mechanics and game implementation (*i.e.* programming) [34, 35], moving away from game narrative's development. In the programming field, toolkits are often used as a way to provide a structure for individuals to develop customized applications, even if they do not have dedicated technical knowledge.

Nelson and Mateas [36] claim that what is preventing users to create their own games is not access to game programming tools but the game design process itself. According to the authors, the process of introducing thematic content (*e.g.* bike safety, algebra) in a logic way while taking advantage of the specific qualities of games (e.g. enabling players to experientially explore rule systems, creating a strong sense of player agency) is one of the major obstacles to game creation. Aiming to fill this gap, authors developed an automated game design system, a creative enhancing tool designed to support game designers with little experience. While the system allows game creators to test a series of concepts and relations by mapping them in terms of game mechanics, it does not explore dimensions such as narrative, history or characters, focusing mostly on defining game mechanics.

Narratives enable the structure of a sense of personality and ambition, and convey values and beliefs [37–39]. In the field of game design, narratives give context to gameplay and may lead to a deeper and emotional engagement of the player with the game experience. Combined and articulated with game mechanics, narrative elements (labelled by Fullerton as *dramatic elements* [40]) such as story, premise and challenge, can contribute to turn games into meaningful experiences.

While writing a story or narrative in the traditional way (*i.e.* pen and paper) involves planning, using text and/or mind maps, writing a game narrative requires more than a simple plan structure, due to several guidelines to follow by. As it is already accepted that the combination of the narrative elements, the interactive character, the challenge and the content present in digital games (*i.e.* defining the story, characters, challenges, rules, among others) is motivating and able to promote behavioural changes [26], game-based narratives can serve as a powerful tool to education in classroom settings, improving and expanding the curriculum whilst encouraging teachers and learners' creativity [6]. Moreover, introducing other forms of writing (*e.g.* multimedia writing) can be seen as a successful way to literacy development, even for reluctant writers or non-writers, [23].

From the toolkits' analysis (*e.g.* [36, 41–45]), to be detailed in a future paper, although addressing game design, somehow neglect or do not pay particular attention to the process of developing game narratives. Other resources, aiming to promote creative thinking and often used in the construction of narratives (*e.g.* idea cards or "trigger cards", small cards with questions whose main purpose is to facilitate the process of creating or refining ideas by questioning the initial idea) disregard game's mechanics and gameplay, and therefore cannot be considered as a solution to be used when defining the structure of a digital game.

3 Creating Narratives Using the Gamers4Nature Toolkit to Game Design

Taking the findings presented in Sect. 2.2. In consideration, and acknowledging the importance of game narrative construction in the design of engaging games, the Gamers4Nature project research team developed a Toolkit to Game Design that encompasses both narrative and gameplay, to be used by younger audiences (upper secondary and undergraduate students), with or without experience in game development during game design sessions. The toolkit was developed based on the premise that individuals without technical knowledge in the game development process can also actively contribute in game design sessions, namely in the process of building and defining narratives.

3.1 The Gamers4Nature Toolkit to Game Design

In the Gamers4Nature Toolkit to Game Design [46], information about game elements and guidelines to create a well-structured game is provided through a Game Construction Cards Set and a Rapid Game Design Document [47, 48]. Focused on supporting the development of games by youngsters to promote environmental awareness, the Toolkit also includes a set of thematic cards addressing nature protection and environment preservation issues.

The Game Construction Cards Set comprises 12 cards addressing one game element: players, objectives, rules, resources, conflicts, outcome, challenge, premise, characters, story, play and dramatic arc. To each card, in the front, a trigger question (*e.g.* Rules card – "What is allowed to do?") and a small explanation (*e.g.* Rules Card – "Rules define what the player can and cannot do") were added; in the back, a description of the game element and examples of its presence in games were given. The cards set follows an adaptation of Fullerton's [40] approach to gameplay and game design, and its development included several stages of validation with experts and potential users [48].

The Rapid Game Design Document, sized A3, was created to support and guide users during the use of the game construction cards. On the left side (Fig. 1), it presents a path to explore the cards, with suggestion on how to define and write the game's narrative; on the right side (Fig. 2), a structural planning sheet that asks users to summarize their game's structure and ideas. Recommendations about the importance of time management and game elements are also provided.

Fig. 1. Rapid Game Design Document (left side, partial view)

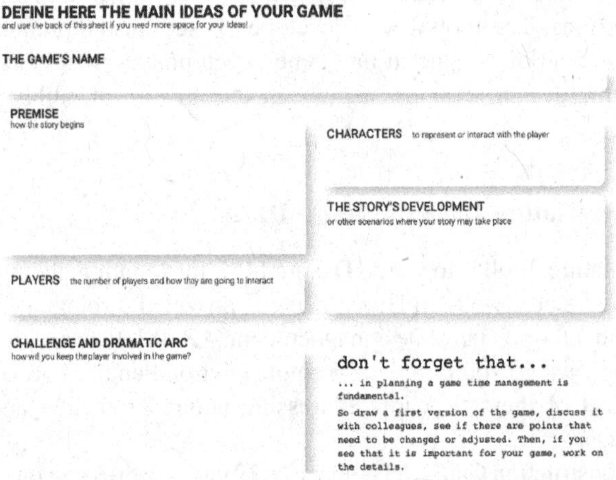

Fig. 2. Rapid Game Design Document (right side, partial view)

While following the Rapid Game Design Document, users are invited to start from defining the game's premise, story and characters, and then move to elements related with challenge, goals, mechanics (procedures and resources), rules and outcomes. Following this first overview of the game elements and their relations, users are asked (on the right side of the document) giving a **name** to the game; to write the **premise**, on how the story starts; to define the number of **players** and how they will interact; to describe the **characters** who will represent or interact with the player. Users may then develop the **story** (from the premise) or introduce other scenarios where the story may take place; after that, an explanation on how the engagement between the player and the game need will be addressed in the **challenge** and **dramatic arc** field. Users are asked to define the **goals**, which, combined with **resources** and **actions**, will influence the gameplay;

rules define what the player can and cannot do; **conflicts** highlight the obstacles that the player will face along the game; and the document ends with defining the **outcome**, that is, how and when the game finishes.

Considering the importance of time management in game development, especially in short-term game design sessions, the Rapid Game Design Document includes a note advising users to draw a first version of the game, to brainstorm and discuss it with coworkers/colleagues, and then to see which points need alteration or improvement. This will advise users/game creators to develop a first functional prototype of the game, to test game's consistency and mechanics and to look for eventual errors, and then – if there is time – to work on an improved version of the game.

3.2 Method

In order to assess the Gamers4Nature Toolkit to Game Design efficiency in supporting the construction of game narratives, namely with audiences with little or no experience in digital game's development, the research team organized two "game narrative design sessions" focused on microplastic pollution, with undergraduate students from a non-ICT (Information and Communication Technologies) course.

Participants. Considering the predominance of ICT students during the Toolkit development and validation process [48], and as the research team aimed to test the toolkit with users with little or no experience in game design, students from a Social Sciences course whose curriculum did not address programming or game design subjects were invited to participate in game narrative creation sessions. 46 undergraduate students (convenience sampling, 11 male and 35 female) participated in the game narrative creation sessions. 33 (73%) were regular players (*i.e.* played digital games on a regular basis), and 3 (6%) already participated in game creation activities. 26 participants (56%) mentioned to prefer to play strategy games, followed by action games (38%, n = 17) and memory games (21%, n = 10).

As for previous knowledge about the theme (*i.e.* microplastic pollution), 14 participants (30%) had already heard about microplastic pollution, 12 (27%) were familiar with the theme and 9 (19%) knew or relatively knew the theme. 7 participants (15%) mentioned that they never heard about microplastic pollution. From the participants' comments shared with the research team, it was possible to notice, when creating the narratives, they got involved with the theme, searching for more information, and demonstrated motivation towards change in habits.

Procedures. The game narrative design sessions took place in October 2019, in classroom environment, conducted by 2 researchers. During these sessions, participants organized themselves in groups and were challenged to use the Toolkit to Game Design to develop a narrative of a game focused on microplastic pollution, one of the thematic cards set provided in the Toolkit. Sessions took 2 h each (one in the morning and the other at the end of the day), and involved the participation of 14 groups, 3 to 4 students per group.

Participants explored the cards set using the Rapid Game Design Document as a guide. After reading the thematic cards information and engaging in a short brainstorm session where the game's theme was discussed, participants were invited to work on the structure of their game's narrative, by following the game design document path. The researchers who oriented the sessions were there to conduct it and to help, if needed, in the exploration of the game resources.

To ensure internal validity, data was collected through triangulation of multiple sources: observation (field notes), Rapid Game Design Document analysis and questionnaires: (i) the first questionnaire, applied at the beginning of the session, asking about participants' gaming habits and previous knowledge about microplastic pollution; and (ii) a questionnaire to evaluate the contribution of the Toolkit to Game Design to the game narratives' writing process.

This last questionnaire contained questions related to the participants' opinion on the toolkit's usability, included an analysis of its strengths, weaknesses, opportunities of use and possible threats (SWOT analysis) and an open field for suggestions.

4   Results and Discussion

Figure 3 presents the information about the narratives developed by the participants during the game narrative creation sessions.

For an easy reading, narratives are grouped according to two variables: environmental focus (that is, the addressed theme) and player mode (single player/multiplayer). The 14 game narratives developed by undergraduate students went from catching or avoiding objects (*e.g.* plastic, microplastic particles, endangered animals) through different landscapes, to platform games, strategy and quizzes.

The results presented in Fig. 3 show that participants tended to develop games narratives for single players, as of the 14 game narratives, 9 were designed to be played only by one player.

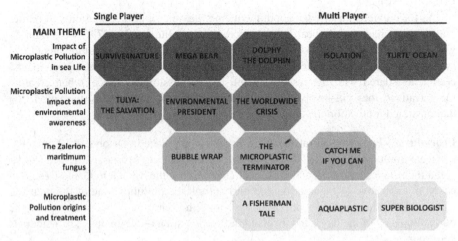

Fig. 3. Name and themes of the games developed by the participants during the game narrative creation sessions

Regarding narrative's themes:

the impact of microplastic pollution in sea life (not directly addressed in the thematic cards) was the theme of 9 narratives;
3 games introduced the *Zalerion maritimum fungus* – a fungus addressed in the thematic cards that, according to recent research [49], is able to biodegrade polyethylene, a source of microplastic pollution – as a hero/weapon to destroy plastic;
3 games focused on microplastic pollution origins and treatment (addressed in the thematic cards);
and 3 games focused on the dangers of microplastic pollution and the importance of developing environmental awareness (addressed in the thematic cards).

During the sessions, focused on the game narrative development, it was possible to see that participants used the information provided in the Gamers4Nature Toolkit's game cards to create the game's structure (*e.g.* player mode, challenge, characters, outcome) and the thematic cards to define the game's narrative, to establish the premise and to set up the story's plot. In what concerns the thematic card that introduces the *Zalerion maritimum* fungus, it was evident that participants read the thematic card and integrated its information in the game's narrative.

Along the sessions, and through the analysis of the information collected via direct observation, it was possible to notice that some participants revealed difficulties when defining the game narrative. While using the Game Design Document, participants revealed some struggles in using the 12 game construction cards, with the main difficulty being the definition and understanding of what "rules" meant. Even though the information presented in the "rules" card stated that rules are what is allowed and not allowed to do in the game, and the role each item represents in the game, several groups asked for help. It was latter evident, through the analysis of participants' game document, that, regardless the researcher's clarifications, participants approached "rules" in different ways: some groups considered character's death, when losing the game, as a rule, while others considered this situation as a possible outcome.

4.1 Participants' Opinion on the Gamers4Nature Toolkit to Game Design

By the end of the session, participants were asked to share their thoughts about the Toolkit contributions to the game narrative creation session by being asked to fill a questionnaire with questions addressing the toolkit's usability and a SWOT analysis.
Collected data analysis indicates that:

89% of the participants agreed that the Toolkit could be used by individuals with and without experience in game development;
83% agreed that using the Toolkit led to less cognitive effort related with content memorization;
83% agreed that the resources included in the Toolkit presented information in a concise way, not disturbing the task they had in hands;
and 73% of the participants agreed that the Toolkit design options (e.g. colours, font size) had no impact in the process of reading and understanding the content it provided.

As for the SWOT (strengths, weaknesses, opportunities [of use] and threats) analysis, when asked to name what were, in their opinion, the Toolkit's strengths, participants mentioned its ease of use either by user with and without previous knowledge about game design, the potential for creativity (*"It's a funny way to learn more about the environment, it's easy to follow"*), the easy reading and understanding of the different steps as being the most positive aspects of the Toolkit to Game Design. Five participants mentioned that the Toolkit's major weakness was the overload of information, as *"There are too many thematic cards"*.

Regarding the Toolkit's opportunities (*i.e.* other scenarios where it could be used), participants acknowledge its suitability for non-experience users during the game construction process; its adaptability, namely the easiness of adapting new content with other themes; the fact that it could be used by younger and older audiences; its potential in educational contexts such as schools, but also in more familiar contexts; the support it provided in situations of lack of creativity or creative block; and, mainly, the fact that it could be used as a dynamic and interesting approach to teaching and learning.

Regarding threats (*i.e.* potential problems arriving from the Toolkit's use or similar products), one participant mentioned that the physical Toolkit (*i.e.* paper cards, document) could fall into disuse when the digital content (*i.e.* the Gamers4Nature project's website[1] that have all the Toolkit's content online) would become available.

14 participants suggested that numbers should be added to the cards, to facilitate its organization in case of shuffle.

5 Final Considerations

Digital games, by presenting learning activities in significant contexts controlled by the learner, have the capability to trigger curiosity and interest towards the educational subject [50]. Moreover, recent research [15, 29] evidences that involving students in the creation of their own games may enhance their interest toward the addressed topic, a sense of ownership and a better understanding of the value of what is learned.

Narratives are an important and motivating element in games. The study presented in this paper indicates that Gamers4Nature Toolkit to Game Design, as it introduces a set of artefacts designed to support game creation activities, was able to ease the game narratives' writing process, namely in sessions with participants with no ICT or game design background. The Rapid Game Design Document was used and explored throughout the game narratives' construction sessions. The Game Construction Cards were also used during that process, and the thematic cards were consulted – even if fewer times – as a source of information and ideas for the game story development.

Preliminary results indicate that the Gamers4Nature Toolkit was able to support users with little or no experience in game design to develop a game narrative, and therefore can be seen as an engaging approach to game narrative's creation, able to be used by different audiences with different skills. Also, it demonstrated the potential of being an alternative and engaging way to learn about the addressed theme.

As the study introduced in this paper was based in a convenience sample, with most participants having no experience in game design and implementation (only 6%

---

[1] http://www.gamers4nature.pt/index.php?lang=EN.

(n = 3) had previous experience in game design), additional game narrative design sessions organized with users with experience in game narratives and game programming will allow the research team to establish comparisons between the two profiles, namely between the session's outputs. New sets of cards are also being developed and validated: game development cards (i.e. coding), designed to assist on the implementation for mobile of the created game narratives; and additional thematic cards, focused on environmental awareness and nature protection. Due to its adaptability, it is expected that the Gamers4Nature Toolkit to Game Design can be adapted to game design sessions addressing themes other than environmental preservation. Therefore, further tests with other themes are also being considered.

Acknowledgments. This work is part of the Gamers4Nature project, PTDC/COM-OUT/031047, that has the financial support of FCT – Foundation for Science and Technology (Portugal)/MCTES – Ministry of Science, Technology and Higher Education and FEDER under the PT2020 agreement.

References

1. Huizinga, J.: Homo ludens: o jogo como elemento da cultura. Perspectiva: São Paulo (2001)
2. Sayre, S., King, C.: Entertainment and Society. Routledge, New York (2010). https://doi.org/10.4324/9780203882931
3. Aarsand, P.A.: Computer and video games in family life: the digital divide as a resource in intergenerational interactions. Childhood **14**(2), 235–256 (2007). https://doi.org/10.1177/0907568207078330
4. Ortet, C.P., Costa, L.V., Veloso, A.I.: Jizo: a gamified digital app for senior cyclo-tourism in the miOne community. In: Zagalo, N., Veloso, A.I., Costa, L., Mealha, Ó. (eds.) VJ 2019. CCIS, vol. 1164, pp. 195–207. Springer, Cham (2019). https://doi.org/10.1007/978-3-030-37983-4_15
5. Barradas, R., Lencastre, J.A.: Gamification e game-based learning: estratégias eficazes para promover a competitividade positiva nos processos de ensino e de aprendizagem. Investigar em Educação. **2**(6), 11–37 (2017)
6. Young, M.F., Slota, S.T., Travis, R., Choi, B.: Game narrative, interactive fiction, and storytelling. In: Video Games and Creativity, pp. 199–222. Elsevier (2015). https://doi.org/10.1016/B978-0-12-801462-2.00010-2
7. Kiili, K.: Digital game-based learning: towards an experiential gaming model. Internet Higher Educ. **8**(1), 13–24 (2005). https://doi.org/10.1016/j.iheduc.2004.12.001
8. Squire, K.: From content to context: videogames as designed experience. Educ. Res. **35**(8), 19–29 (2006). https://doi.org/10.3102/0013189X035008019
9. Vandercruysse, S., Vandewaetere, M., Clarebout, G.: Game-based learning: a review on the effectiveness of educational games. In: Cruz-Cunha, M.M. (ed.) Handbook of Research on Serious Games as Educational, Business and Research Tools, pp. 628–647. IGI Global (2012). https://doi.org/10.4018/978-1-4666-0149-9.ch032
10. Gee, J.P.: What video games have to teach us about learning and literacy. Comput. Entertain. **1**(1), 20–20 (2003). https://doi.org/10.1145/950566.950595
11. Jenkins, H.: Confronting the Challenges of Participatory Culture: Media Education for the 21st Century. The MIT Press, Cambridge (2009). https://doi.org/10.7551/mitpress/8435.001.0001

12. Selander, S.: Designs for learning and ludic engagement. Digital Creativ. **19**(3), 145–152 (2008). https://doi.org/10.1080/14626260802312673

13. Ke, F.: An implementation of design-based learning through creating educational computer games: a case study on mathematics learning during design and computing. Comput. Educ. **73**, 26–39 (2014)

14. Howland, K., Good, J.: Learning to communicate computationally with Flip: a bi-modal programming language for game creation. Comput. Educ. **80**, 224–240 (2015)

15. Falcão, T.P., Peres, F.N., de Morais, D.C.S., Oliveira, G.S.: Participatory methodologies to promote student engagement in the development of educational digital games. Comput. Educ. **116**, 161–175 (2018)

16. Murray, J.H.: Toward a cultural theory of gaming: digital games and the co-evolution of media, mind, and culture. Popular Commun. **4**(3), 185–202 (2006). https://doi.org/10.1207/s15405710pc0403_3

17. Griffiths, M.D., Davies, M.N.O.: Research noteExcessive online computer gaming: implications for education.: research note. J. Comput. Assist. Learn. **18**(3), 379–380 (2002). https://doi.org/10.1046/j.0266-4909.2002.00248.x

18. Ferguson, C.J.: The good, the bad and the ugly: a meta-analytic review of positive and negative effects of violent video games. Psych. Q. **78**(4), 309–316 (2007). https://doi.org/10.1007/s11126-007-9056-9

19. Merhi, O., Faugloire, E., Flanagan, M., Stoffregen, T.A.: Motion sickness, console video games, and head-mounted displays. Human Fact. J. Human Factors Ergon. Soc. **49**(5), 920–934 (2007). https://doi.org/10.1518/001872007X230262

20. Connoly, T., Boyle, E., MacArthur, E., Hainey, T., Boyle, J.: A systematic literature review of empirical evidence on computer games and serious games. Comput. Educ. **59**, 661–686 (2012)

21. El Rhalibi, A., Tian, F., Pan, Z., Liu, B. (eds.): Edutainment 2016. LNCS, vol. 9654. Springer, Cham (2016). https://doi.org/10.1007/978-3-319-40259-8

22. Jeffrey, E.: Game making for learning: a systematic review of the research literature. In: 8th International Conference of Education, Research and Innovation, Seville (Spain) (2015)

23. Robertson, J., Good, J.: Children's narrative development through computer game authoring. TechTrends **49**(5), 43–59 (2005). https://doi.org/10.1007/BF02763689

24. Gros, B.: Digital games in education: the design of games-based learning environments. J. Res. Technol. Educ. **40**(1), 23–38 (2007). https://doi.org/10.1080/15391523.2007.10782494

25. Jarvin, L.: Edutainment, games, and the future of education in a digital world: edutainment, games, and the future of education in a digital world. New Direct. Child Adolesc. Develop. **2015**(147), 33–40 (2015). https://doi.org/10.1002/cad.20082

26. De Grove, F., Bourgonjon, J., Van Looy, J.: Digital games in the classroom? A contextual approach to teachers' adoption intention of digital games in formal education. Comput. Human Behav. **28**(6), 2023–2033 (2012). https://doi.org/10.1016/j.chb.2012.05.021

27. Giannakos, M.N., Jaccheri, L.: From players to makers: An empirical examination of factors that affect creative game development. Int. J. Child-Comput. Interact. **18**, 27–36 (2018). https://doi.org/10.1016/j.ijcci.2018.06.002

28. Baytak, A., Land, S.M.: A case study of educational game design by kids and for kids. Proc. Soc. Behav. Sci. **2**(2), 5242–5246 (2010). https://doi.org/10.1016/j.sbspro.2010.03.853

29. Huizinga, J., Ten Dam, G., Voogt, J., Admiraal, W.: Teacher perceptions of the value of game-based learning in secondary education. Comput. Educ. **110**, 105–115 (2017)

30. Papavlasopoulou, S., Giannakos, M.N., Jaccheri, L.: Exploring children's learning experience in constructionism-based coding activities through design-based research. Comput. Human Behav. **99**, 415–427 (2019). https://doi.org/10.1016/j.chb.2019.01.008

31. Greenberg, S.: Toolkits and interface creativity. Multimed. Tools App. **32**(2), 139–159 (2007). https://doi.org/10.1007/s11042-006-0062-y

32. Oulasvirta, A., Hornbaek, K.: HCI research as problem-solving. In: Proceedings of the 2016 CHI Conference on Human Factors in Computing Systems (CHI 2016), NY, ACM, pp. 4956–4967 (2016)

33. Ledo, D., Houben, S., Vermeulen, J., Marquardt, N., Oehlberg, L., Greenberg, S.: Evaluation strategies for HCI toolkit research. In: Proceedings of the 2018 CHI Conference on Human Factors in Computing Systems – CHI 2018 (2018)

34. Abdullah, N.A., Kamaruddin, R.H.R.A., Razak, Z., Yousoff, Z.B.M.: A toolkit design framework for authoring multimedia game-oriented. In: Eighth IEEE International Conference on Advanced Learning Technologies (2008)

35. Nadolski, R.J., et al.: EMERGO: a methodology and toolkit for developing serious games in higher education. Simul. Gaming. **39**, 338–352 (2007)

36. Nelson, M.J., Mateas, M.: An interactive game-design assistant. In: IUI 2008: Proceedings of the 13th International Conference on Intelligent User Interfaces (2008)

37. Barthes, F.: The Pleasure of the Text. Noonday Press, New York (1975)

38. Howard, G.S.: Culture tales: a narrative approach to thinking, cross-cultural psychology, and psychotherapy. Am. Psychol. **46**(3), 187–197 (1991). https://doi.org/10.1037/0003-066X.46.3.187

39. Mills, C., Pawson, K.: Integrating motivation, risk-taking and self-identity: a typology of ICT enterprise development narratives. Int. Small Bus. J. Res. Entrepr. **30**(5), 584–606 (2011). https://doi.org/10.1177/0266242610390594

40. Fullerton, T.: Game Design Workshop: A Playcentric Approach to Creating Innovative Games (2008)

41. Piller, F., Ihl, C., Fuller, J., Stotkdo, C.: Toolkits for open innovation - the case of mobile phone games. In: Proceedings of the 37th Hawaii International Conference on System Sciences (2004)

42. Heussner, T.: The Game Narrative Toolbox. Routledge (2015). https://doi.org/10.4324/9781315766836

43. Kafai, Y.B.: Minds in Play: Computer Game Design as a Context for Children's Learning. Routledge, NY (2009)

44. Kafai, Y.B., Burke, Q.: Connected Code: Why Children Need to Learn Programming. The MIT Press, London (2014)

45. Ho, X., Tomitsch, M.: Affordances of brainstorming toolkits and their use in game jams. In: Proceedings of the 14th International Conference on the Foundations of Digital Games, San Luis Obispo, CA (2019)

46. Beça, P., Aresta, M., Santos, R., Veloso, A.I., Gomes, G., Pereira, M.: Supporting the game construction process: development of artefacts in the context of a toolkit to game design. In: Zagalo, N., Veloso, A.I., Costa, L., Mealha, Ó. (eds.) VJ 2019. CCIS, vol. 1164, pp. 99–110. Springer, Cham (2019). https://doi.org/10.1007/978-3-030-37983-4_8

47. Beça, P., Aresta, M., Ortet, C., Santos, R., Veloso, A., Ribeiro, S.: Promoting student engagement in the design of digital games: the creation of games using a toolkit to game design. In: 2020 IEEE 20th International Conference on Advanced Learning Technologies (ICALT), Tartu, pp. 98–102 (2020)

48. Beça, P., et al.: Developing a toolkit to game design - the Gamers4Nature project: from concept to artefact. In: 15th Conference on the Foundations of Digital Games (FDG), Malta (2020)

49. Paço, A., et al.: Biodegradation of polyethylene microplastics by the marine fungus Zalerion maritimum. Sci. Total Environ. **586**, 10–15 (2017). https://doi.org/10.1016/j.scitotenv.2017.02.017

50. Vos, N., van der Meijden, H., Denessen, E.: Effects of constructing versus playing an educational game on student motivation and deep learning strategy use. Comput. Educ. **56**, 127–137 (2011)

Reward-Mediated Individual and Altruistic Behavior

Samuel Gomes[1]([⊠]) [iD], Tomás Alves[1] [iD], João Dias[2] [iD], and Carlos Martinho[1] [iD]

[1] INESC-ID and Instituto Superior Técnico, University of Lisbon, Lisbon, Portugal
samuel.gomes@tecnico.ulisboa.pt
[2] INESC-ID and Faculty of Sciences and Technology, University of Algarve, Faro, Portugal

Abstract. Recent research has taken a particular interest in observing the dynamics between individual and altruistic behavior. This is a commonly approached problem when reasoning about social dilemmas, which have a plethora of real-world counterparts in the fields of education, health, and economics. Weighing how incentives influence in-game behavior, our study examines individual and altruistic interactions in the context of a game task, by analyzing the players' strategies and interaction motives when facing different reward attribution functions. Consequently, a model for interaction motives is proposed, with the premise that the motives for interactions can be defined as a continuous space, ranging from self-oriented (associated with individual behaviors) to others-oriented (associated with altruistic behaviors). To evaluate the promotion of individual and altruistic behavior, we leverage Message Across, an *in-loco* two-player videogame with adaptable score attribution systems. We conducted a user testing phase ($N = 66$) to verify to what extent individual and altruistic score functions led players to vary their strategies and interaction motives orientations. Our results indicate that both of these metrics varied significantly and according to our expectations, leading us to believe in the suitability of applying an incentive-based strategy to moderate the emergence of in-game behavior perceivable as individual or altruistic.

Keywords: Interaction style · Reward system · Message Across · Serious games · Behavior promotion

1 Introduction

Since the last century, researchers have studied the dynamics between individual and altruistic behavior [10, 14]. This aspect is an important target of analysis in social dilemma implementations, such as the prisoner's dilemma [16, 22] or the public goods game [6, 12, 20]. In these scenarios, subjects have to decide between acting with self or collective interest, thus focusing or not in the development of others' welfare. Along social dilemmas, this *self and others* paradigm is also predominant in education. Namely, the theory of Self-determination [4, 21, 23] distinguishes between several levels of motivation, such as intrinsic motivation - related to self definition of goals and satisfaction from self development, and extrinsic motivation – influenced by external factors like rewards, approval or competition.

I. Barbedo et al. (Eds.): VJ 2020, CCIS 1531, pp. 84–97, 2022.
https://doi.org/10.1007/978-3-030-95305-8_7

Over the years, research on behavior promotion has taken particular interest in the use of games to change players' long-term commitments [3, 24, 27], for instance, to develop environment sustainability awareness [15, 19] or non-sedentary behaviors [1, 9]. As an interactive medium, games allow the promotion of feelings of competence through feedback and rewards, and support relatedness through social interactions such as competition and cooperation [21]. Therefore, we credit that promoting in-game behavior can be a useful path to approach aspects of attitude change such as the motives which drive interactions, given the growing impact of games in players' lives [2]. This line of research can help to inspire the parameterization of systems aiming to balance or enhance individual and altruistic facets of behavior among people with different individual or cultural backgrounds, as these intrinsic characteristics might be able to drive distinct game strategies [20]. Researchers have focused on studying how the attribution of different rewards (ranging from simple scores to collectibles, resources, item granting systems, achievement systems, feedback messages, etc.) [4, 11] affect player experience. In fact, although some studies embraced reward-based behavior promotion, there is the consensus that further research in the motives upon interpersonal choice behavior is still needed [16, 28]. Altogether, this work contemplates the following research question:

How can rewards be used to mediate individual and altruistic in-game behavior?

In particular, our hypothesis is that, by changing in-game rewards, we can alter the behaviors of players at an in-game task level. The rewards are, in our case, simply an instrument used to guide players towards an individual or altruistic behavior, as perceived in the context of a task. In other words, they act as incentives for players to engage in certain in-game behaviors.

To answer this problem, we define a model for interaction motives orientation and implemented it in Message Across, an *in-loco* two-player word matching game, with two versions of the score attribution system, aimed at orienting the players' interactions to either themselves or others. In the particular example of Message Across, the task is the completion of a word. Using this game, we conducted user tests where pairs of participants played the different versions without knowing what score systems were being deployed at each moment. We extracted the players' strategies and scores, as well as their self-reported orientation of interaction motives (between self-oriented and others-oriented) to find answers to our research question.

The remaining of the paper is organized as follows: in the next sections, we explore several interaction styles, as well as techniques to promote in-game behavior; then, we describe how we implemented individual and altruistic Message Across versions; afterwards, we include the evaluation process, and present and discuss the empirical results; finally, we summarize the work and finish with future directions.

2 From Theory to a Model of Interaction Motives

We started our analysis by observing which behavior mediation techniques were identified in social dilemmas scenarios. A significant amount of research deploying social dilemmas focuses on collaborative interactions, studying how can higher levels of cooperation and altruism be fostered. Hilbe et al. [12] theoretically examined several strategies to sustain cooperation in the public goods game and volunteers social dilemma, including generalized variants of Tit-for-Tat and Win-Stay Lose-Shift. More importantly, to define such strategies, the authors identified three particular sub-classes of strategies: (i) the fair-neutral strategy which ensures individual payoff is aligned with the average pay-off of the other group members; (ii) the extortionate strategy which, in scenarios where mutual defection leads to the lowest group payoff, is based on ensuring that individual payoffs are above average (related to free-riding and individual focus, not concerning for the others); and (iii) the generous strategy which, in scenarios where mutual coop-eration is the social optimum, consists in letting co-players gain higher payoffs. We find extortionate and generous strategies inspiring in mixed interactions, as they reflect two opposite poles. In one pole, there is an individual motive for interaction, devaluing attention for others, and in the other pole there is an others-oriented motive for interac-tion, devaluing self consequences. Following this line of thought, we further analyzed theories regarding these two opposite ideas.

Hoping to exclusively study individual motives for interaction, we analyzed sev-eral work regarding self-improvement. Self-Improvement can be defined as a conscious desire to improve self ability [25], a result of self evaluation. Numerous research focused on what can influence this behavior, and how it emerges [5, 14, 18, 25]. Task-based scenarios as games may ease the emergence of self-improvement, as task-related self-enhancement – the tendency to maintain positive self-regard – seems to effectively facilitate action taking and overall task performance, as opposed to non task-related self-enhancement [14, 18]. Following this line of thought, we believe that multiplayer games might foster self-improvement through their actions, by rewarding players when embracing choices which individually improve themselves, without directly taking into consideration the actions of other players.

In order to study others-oriented motives for interaction, we examined multiple theories related to altruism. Seelig and Rosof present several categorizations and review several research regarding altruism [26], from which we highlight Kitayama's scale of altruism as masochism [13]. On a study related to the dual nature of the feminine ideal in Japanese culture, the author defines altruism as a continuum between two facets. While the first facet can be interpreted as an interaction consisting of mutual help between peers, the second facet happens when people feel that it is important to do good for others, even if it means the process will not be pleasant for them. In other words, people engaging in the second type of altruism are *exclusively* motivated by others, without even trying to minimize the negative consequences that helping others might bring to themselves. Although some research, such as the works just presented, also associate this effect to *Pathological Altruism*, we will refer to this interaction style as *Extreme Altruism*. We believe that multiplayer games might reflect this interaction style through their actions as well, by rewarding players when embracing choices which exclusively improve others.

2.1   Model of Interaction Motives

Related research allowed us to extract two extreme behaviors: *Self-Improvement* and *Extreme Altruism*. In this work we deploy both these ends of the spectrum, placing them as opposite poles of a continuous interactions motive space (Fig. 1). This space allows us to examine to what extent players interactions are individually or altruistically motivated. In one pole, we have a **Self-oriented** motive for interaction, devaluing attention for others, and in the other pole there is an **Others-oriented** motive for interaction, without valuing self consequences. Based on this interaction motives model, we deemed that an adequate indicator of the emergence of individual and altruistic behavior (besides verifying players' game strategies and final scores) was to acquire self-reported motives for interaction, comprehended between **Self-oriented** and **Others-oriented**.

Interaction Motives

Self. I.   **E. Altr.**

Self- **oriented**   **Others-** **oriented**

Fig. 1. Continuous space organizing interaction motives, between Self-oriented and Others-oriented. Self-oriented motives can be associated to the *Self-Improvement* behavior, and Others-oriented motives can be associated to *Extreme Altruism*.

2.2 Mediating Individual and Altruistic In-Game Behavior

After constructing our interaction motives model, we examined work specifically devoted to behavior promotion. For instance, Vegt et al. [28] showed that, while subjects played a multiplayer game in separate rooms, different game rules could generate distinct reported player experiences and observable distinct player behaviors, further discriminated into four patterns: expected patterns of helping and ignoring, and unexpected patterns of agreeing and obstructing. Returning to social dilemma scenarios, Rosen and Haaga [22] managed to induce higher levels of cooperation in small groups of four to eight subjects playing a prisoner's dilemma (higher number of cooperative game actions, and higher altruistic attitudes toward a specific dilemma story), by applying message-based persuasion methods. To facilitate cooperation, instead of neutrally defining the nature of the dilemma, two explanations were applied: either the positive effects of collaboration and negative effects of free-riding were directly exposed for the considered social dilemma problem; or subjects were told that the same task was presented to various professionals at a conflict-resolution conference, who agreed that *cooperation was the only appropriate response to the conflict and was necessary for societal harmony in general*. Galbiati and Vertova on the other hand, studied the promotion of cooperation in a repeated public goods game through contribution obligations - the minimum each player had to contribute to the public good to have a chance of being rewarded [6]. The authors concluded that although obligations *per se* could not sustain cooperation over time, higher obligations led players, in average, to focus more in cooperating, while not reducing as much their cooperative contributions through the course of the game. Also, unexpected obligation increases meant cooperation levels increases. Following our research question, we also analyzed several game-oriented reward attribution approaches which we believe to be suitable for in-game behavior promotion, ranging from simple scores to collectibles, resources, item granting systems, achievement systems, player dossiers, and feedback messages [4, 11, 17, 21]. In particular, rewards in the form of scores awaken interest, as they are simple to deploy and allow easy comparisons between players [11, 16, 21]. For instance, McClintock et al. showed that players choices (and possibly the dominance of motives behind such choices) could be manipulated in a modified prisoner's dilemma game, by varying the score display methodology (display of own outcome or both own and other player's outcome) and monetary reward parameters [16]. Notably, more competitive behavior was observed when players were able to compare their and others' scores and in a low – as opposed to a high-reward condition, even though players were separated via a visual barrier and disallowed to communicate. Besides their simple deployment, scores also provide flexibility when parameterizing behavior, as they may not directly influence the way game actions and mechanics operate for a player to progress in a task. Thus, we chose this route for behavior promotion.

3 Solution Description

As previously commented, we used a game called Message Across[1] (Fig. 2) to examine the dynamics of players' interactions. In the course of the game, players try to complete words as they advance through the levels. Each level presents two words on the top of the screen, one for each player. Because we wanted words which were easily understood and completed, only four letter words with two letters in common were considered in our experiments. In the middle of the screen, the game presents a track containing three lanes where letters move towards players. The track also contains two markers, one for each player, arranged at the bottom.

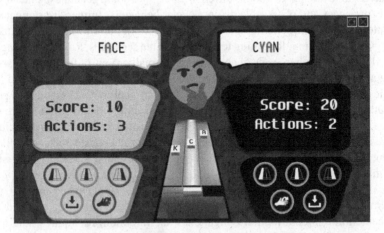

Fig. 2. Screenshot of the game message across.

In order to select a letter, a player has to move his/her marker to the lane where the letter is sliding, and select an action. When the letter collides with the marker, the

---

[1] The implementation of the game is available online, hosted in the platform *GitHub*: https://git hub.com/SamGomes/message-across.

selected action is performed. If two players are in the same lane, only the first player that selects an action is able to perform it. Players can perform one of two possible actions at each moment. They can either **take the letter** or **give the letter** to the other player. The objective of each player is to **obtain the highest score**. In our experiments, each player could perform a maximum of four actions per level, and a level finished whenever both players had no actions left to perform. We believe that a limit of four possible actions exacerbated the players' need to search for meaningful strategies.

After reviewing related research, we built a model for interaction motives bounded between *Self-Improvement* and *Extreme Altruism*. To foster these two extreme behaviors in-game, we developed two divergent scoring versions:

- The **Self-Improvement** version exclusively rewarded 10 points to players who took letters that were useful for them;
- The **Extremely Altruistic** version exclusively rewarded 10 points to players who gave letters needed by the other players.

The duality between these strategies is apparent, as the first rewards players which act for their own task completion, disregarding the actions of other players, while the second one rewards players who exclusively help in others' task completion. Given that these reward versions were developed to allow players to understand the game in different manners, we predicted two distinct trends, which we translated to two hypotheses. Firstly, the players would embrace different, opposite strategies. These strategies would then allow the game to orient the players' interactions towards the opposite poles defined in our interaction motives model:

H1: The Self-Improvement version will implicitly drive players to perform a high number of takes and the Extremely Altruistic version will drive players to perform a high number of gives.

H2: The Self-Improvement version will implicitly drive players to report self-oriented interaction motives, and the Extremely Altruistic version will implicitly drive players to report others-oriented interaction motives.

4   Experimental Setup

In order to evaluate the effectiveness of our approach, we performed several experiments, approved by the Ethics committee of our institute, where pairs of participants played through the different versions of Message Across. In each test, the game versions were obfuscated by using letters to represent them, and the order of presentation of the game versions was uniformly randomized between groups to avoid any potential learning effects. **Therefore, throughout the session, the participants did not know how the game was being scored and had to figure that out by themselves.**

A touch screen was included in the experiment room for players to interact with the game. Two computers were used for our experiments: one computer executed the game and other computer allowed players to self-report their interaction motives orientation through a questionnaire. A Go-Pro video camera[2] was also included for observing player movements and in-game activity and to help remedy some possible inconsistencies in

---

[2] https://gopro.com/en/us/

automatic data collection. The camera was attached to a tripod and positioned approximately 50 cm in front of the touch screen. The camera view of our setup can be observed in Fig. 3.

4.1 Sample

Participants were recruited through standard convenience sampling procedures including direct contact and word of mouth. Subjects included anyone interested in participating if they were at least 18 years old. There were no potential risks and no anticipated benefits to individual participants. We conducted a total of 37 tests in a college laboratory. Participation was open to outside visitors, which meant that not all participants were college students. After data analysis, four tests did not meet quality criteria, e.g. in-game data not recorded or questionnaires with missing answers. Thus, our final data set comprised 33 tests, a total of 66 participants (37 males, 29 females) between 18 and 40 years old ($M = 23.12$; $SD = 4.09$).

4.2 Procedure

The experiment operated as follows: (i) Firstly, participants were informed about the experiment and invited to sign a mandatory consent form. They were also informed that they could stop the experiment at any time; (ii) After signing the consent form, both participants were asked to move next to the touchscreen (as seen in Fig. 3) and received a tutorial regarding in-game mechanics and possible actions to perform. Additionally, participants were allowed to play up to seven levels without being rewarded for any *give* or *take* action, in order to support the development of fluent playing skills; (iii) When both participants felt comfortable with the game mechanics, they played the two game versions in random order with each gaming session requiring the completion of seven levels. After each gaming session, participants were asked to complete questionnaires measuring their interaction motives orientation regarding that session. At the end of the experiment, participants received a candy bar as a compensation for their time.

Fig. 3. Camera view of a group playing Message Across during our experiments.

4.3 Variables

One independent variable was considered, **Score Attribution System** with two possible values: {*Self.I., E.Altr.*}. Three dependent (within-subjects) variables were considered:

- **Mean number of takes**, the mean number of letters a player acquired for him-self/herself in each level. The value space is [0, 4], as each player could perform at most four actions (gives or takes) per level. This variable was measured by analyzing game logs;
- **Final game score**, the score a player obtained at the end of playing each version of the game. This variable was acknowledged to support the differences observed by the mean number of takes, and was obtained through the game logs as well;
- **Interaction motives orientation**, which measured the orientation of motives behind a player's interactions, between self-oriented and others-oriented. This measure was obtained at the end of each played version, through a question "Who did I focus while playing this version?", answered using a seven-point Likert scale ranging from "Me" to "The other player". In our data analysis, we considered a value range between [-3,3], in which -3 symbolized full self-oriented, and 3 symbolized full others-oriented interaction motives.

5 Results

5.1 Mean Number of Takes and Final Score

The distribution of mean number of takes is plotted in Fig. 4. Shapiro-Wilk tests reported a non-normal distribution regarding the mean number of takes values. Therefore, a Wilcoxon paired signed-rank test was performed to compare the two score systems, at the level of significance $p = 0.05$. The number of performed take actions changed highly significantly between the two score strategies, with a large effect size ($Z = 7.06$, $p < < 0.001$, $r = 0.87$). Furthermore, if we analyze the distribution of the data, we can observe that players of *Self-Improvement* score systems performed, on average, a high (near maximum) number of takes ($M \approx 3.64$, $Mdn \approx 3.86$, $SD \approx 0.37$), while oppositely, players of the *Extremely Altruistic* score system performed a low number of takes ($M \approx 0.58$, $Mdn \approx 0.57$, $SD \approx 0.42$). Even though the differences are clearly noticeable, we can also observe that the *Self-Improvement* data is closer to the maximum number of takes, than the altruistic version is to the minimum. Based on our experiments' observations, we argue that this effect was possibly caused by the fact that while searching for the most rewarding strategies, players found easier or more natural to start by taking letters for themselves, which resulted in differences in the final scores, notably slightly higher *Self-Improvement* values (Fig. 5). This tendency may also relate to the assumptions which players initially make of the game (in this game, they might initially be compelled to compete). This trend should be more extensively explored in future studies. *In summary, these results support that players implicitly understood that the optimal strategy while playing the Self-Improvement version was to take letters, and the optimal strategy while playing the Extremely Altruistic version was to give letters, even though these strategies were unknown throughout the game execution. However, while playing the game, the players seemed compelled to take letters for themselves in both conditions, which may relate to their initial assumptions.*

5.2 Interaction Motives Orientation

The distribution of the interaction motive orientation values is plotted in Fig. 6. Shapiro-Wilk tests reported a non-normal distribution regarding the motives orientation values. Therefore, a Wilcoxon paired signed-rank test was conducted, at the level of significance $p = 0.05$. The motive orientation values also varied highly significantly between the two score attribution strategies, with a large effect size ($Z = -5.73$, $p < < 0.001$, $r = 0.71$). By observing the distribution of the data, we can conclude that *Self-Improvement* responses were driven towards "Self-oriented" ($M \approx -1.76$, $Mdn = -2$, $SD \approx 1.43$), opposite to *Extreme Altruism* responses, which were approximated towards "Others-oriented" ($M \approx 1.12$, $Mdn = 2$, $SD \approx 2.30$). However, similar to the aforementioned results, there was a natural tendency for the players of *Extreme Altruism* to deviate from the expected value range, in this case the full "Others-oriented" motives, which may also have been an effect of the players' initial assumptions. *Summing up, these results indicate that, as expected, the Self-Improvement version was perceived as allowing players to improve their gameplay, and the Extremely Altruistic score system was perceived as a helping scenario implying that players' interactions were motivated by other players. However, these results reflected a natural tendency for Extreme Altruism players to deviate from the expected, full "Others-oriented" motives, which may also relate to their initial assumptions.*

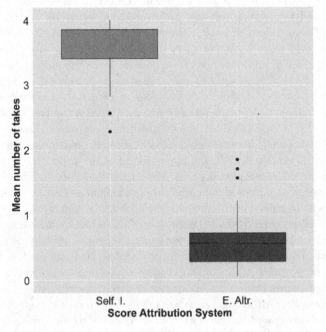

Fig. 4. Distribution of mean number of takes by score system.

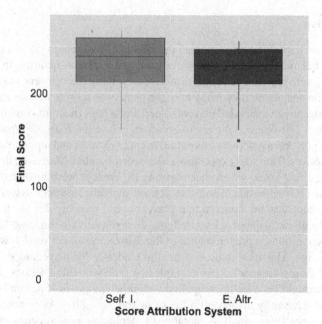

Fig. 5. Distribution of final scores by score system.

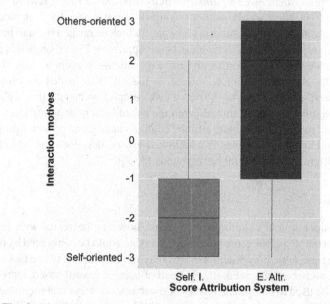

Fig. 6. Distribution of interaction motives orientation values by score system.

5.3 Discussion

In this study we deployed and compared the effects of two score systems, representing two extreme behavior styles: *Self-Improvement* and *Extreme Altruism*, in the players strategies and self-reported interaction motives. Notably, the players played through several game levels, without knowing how the game was scored. Results indicated that the *Self-Improvement* version led players to perform a high (near maximum) number of takes and report self-oriented interaction motives, while the *Extreme Altruism* version led players to perform a low (near minimum) number of takes and report others-oriented interaction motives. Thus, our expectations were corroborated. Moreover, the tendencies revealed high effect sizes, which means strong differences were mediated by the two score functions. It is important to note that rich and dynamic interactions were promoted, even though there was the concern that players could possibly deviate their focus to the game tasks alone, without acknowledging their rewards (in this case, their scores). Still, in both conditions, a predominance of the *Self-Improvement* version was observed over all measures. This may indicate a natural tendency for players to start exploring the effects of their own actions, before exploring others-oriented actions. Also, in this game, players might be initially compelled to compete, a possible reason being that all scores were concurrently displayed in the game interface [16]. As commented before, this trend requires future analysis, notably by deploying new versions of our game. Nevertheless, the aforementioned results reflect an important finding, which answers our hypotheses and research question: *our score attribution strategies led all players to implicitly adopt significantly different in-game strategies (mean number of takes) and to report different interaction motive orientations for the two game versions, aligned to each behavior pole. Thus, evidence was obtained for individual and altruistic reward mediated in-game behavior.* In other words, without using different game items or mechanics, players still managed to learn meaningful strategies, which motivated them to interact in different ways, thus proving the effectiveness of our approach. Even though this may not necessarily indicate that, while performing our experiments, players were intrinsically less selfish in the altruistic condition, results do indicate that in this condition, they were more focused on the other player from a task completion perspective. Taking that into account, we still believe that this research may shed light in applying individual or altruistic-oriented rewards to facilitate attitude change via in-game behavior promotion, or to regulate and balance dilemmas in which the players' decisions can be influenced by individual differences or cultural backgrounds [8, 20].

5.4 Limitations

The further consideration of a similar strategy must, however, be treated with care, as in order to apply our strategy, our game presented tasks that could be completed by different means, but using the same player actions. This may not be the case of the tasks present in all games. In more complex scenarios, instead of using a reward-based approach *per se*, rewards can be used to complement rules or mechanics in ways that might be further investigated in different serious games and social dilemmas scenarios, while trying to avoid player assumption biases. Finally, for experiment ease, we acknowledged just two types of actions, contrasting with most modern games that include a wider range of action possibilities. The fact that only four actions were allowed at each level may have limited the emergence of interactions as well.

6 Conclusions

In this work we approached the promotion of behaviors perceivable as individual or altruistic, exclusively through the use of rewards as scores. Our premise was that an individual behavior, modeled by a full self-directed interaction motive orientation, could be implicitly incentivized by rewarding players who contributed to the completion of their own tasks, while, oppositely, an altruistic behavior, modeled by a full others-directed interaction motive orientation, could be implicitly incentivized by rewarding players who contributed to the completion of other players' tasks.

To test the validity of these assumptions, we deployed two different score attribution systems in a word-matching game named Message Across, and conducted several user tests, where participants did not know how the games were scored. The evaluation comprehended two main aspects: the first was to verify if there was an actual change in the players' task completion strategies, and the second was to acquire and compare the players' perception of who they were focusing on while playing the game.

The results indicated accentuated tendencies for the promotion of both individual and altruistic in-game behavior, as highly significant differences, aligned to our expectations, were observed for the players' strategies and self-reported interaction motive orientations. In particular, an individual score function drove players to perform a high number of takes and an altruistic function drove players to perform a low number of takes. Besides, these diverging players' strategies allowed the individual version to motivate players to focus on themselves, and the altruistic version to motivate players to focus on other players. While this does not necessarily indicate that players were less selfish in the altruistic condition, results indicate that in this condition, players were more focused on the other player from a task completion perspective.

Future research includes the investigation of whether individual differences such as personality have an effect on how people vary their playing strategies and interaction motives when a game targets to mediate individual or altruistic behavior. We also believe that varying the number of actions per level, words size and using different numbers of shared letters is worthwhile to verify how the length and type of the task can have an impact on interactions and playing styles. A cross cultural study would also be interesting, given the already presented tendency for culture to influence players' strategies and behavior evaluations [8, 20]. Besides, we can verify what differences may emerge when separating players, restricting their interactions [16, 28], or extend our analysis by contemplating interactions styles beyond the ones considered in the present study, such as mutual help or competition. Finally, our findings also contribute to the field of automatic education and training, due to the importance of behavior promotion for this research topic. Models such as GIMME [7], that aim to optimize the collective ability of groups interacting with one another, may use scores to mediate students' interactions, thus empowering collective teaching in multiplayer game settings. Furthermore, promoting interactions using rewards allows researchers to take a more human approach to the integration of agents that simulate people in serious games, besides adding expressiveness to their simulation models.

Acknowledgments. This work was supported by national funds through Fundação para a Ciência e a Tecnologia (FCT) with references SFRH/BD/143460/2019, SFRH/BD/144798/2019, and UIDB/50021/2020.

References

1. Arundell, L., Parker, K., Salmon, J., Veitch, J., Timperio, A.: Informing behaviour change: what sedentary behaviours do families perform at home and how can they be targeted? Int. J. Environ. Res. Publ. Health **16**, 4565 (2019). https://doi.org/10.3390/ijerph16224565
2. Chatfield, T.: Fun Inc Why Gaming Will Dominate the Twenty-First Century. Pegasus Books, Oakland (2010)
3. Chow, C.Y., Riantiningtyas, R.R., Kanstrup, M.B., Papavasileiou, M., Liem, G.D., Olsen, A.: Can games change children's eating behaviour? A review of gamification and serious games. Food Qual. Prefer. **80**, 103823 (2020). https://doi.org/10.1016/j.foodqual.2019.103823, http://www.sciencedirect.com/science/article/pii/S0950329319302964
4. Cruz, C., Hanus, M.D., Fox, J.: The need to achieve: Players' perceptions and uses of extrinsic meta-game reward systems for video game consoles. Comput. Human Behav. **71**, 516–524 (2017). https://doi.org/10.1016/j.chb.2015.08.017, http://www.sciencedirect.com/science/article/pii/S0747563215300960
5. Dunn, T.G., Shriner, C.: Deliberate practice in teaching: what teachers do for self-improvement. Teach. Teach. Educ. **15**(6), 631–651 (1999). doi: https://doi.org/10.1016/S0742-051X(98)00068-7, http://www.sciencedirect.com/science/article/pii/S0742051X98000687
6. Galbiati, R., Vertova, P.: Obligations and cooperative behaviour in public good games. Games Econ. Behav. **64**(1), 146–170 (2008). https://doi.org/10.1016/j.geb.2007.09.004, http://www.sciencedirect.com/science/article/pii/S0899825607001650
7. Gomes, S., Dias, J., Martinho, C.: Gimme: Group interactions manager for multiplayer serious games. In: 2019 IEEE Conference on Games (CoG), pp. 1–8 (2019). https://doi.org/10.1109/CIG.2019.8847962
8. Hagger, M.S., Rentzelas, P., Koch, S.: Evaluating group member behaviour under individualist and collectivist norms: a cross-cultural comparison. Small Group Res. **45**(2), 217–228 (2014)
9. Hagood, D., Ching, C.C., Schaefer, S.: Integrating physical activity data in videogames with user-centered dashboards. In: Proceedings of the Sixth International Conference on Learning Analytics & Knowledge. p. 530–531. LAK 2016, Association for Computing Machinery, New York, NY, USA (2016). https://doi.org/10.1145/2883851.2883958
10. Hamilton, W.D.: The evolution of altruistic behavior. Am. Nat. **97**(896), 354–356 (1963). https://doi.org/10.1086/497114
11. Hao, W., Chuen-Tsai, S.: Game reward systems: Gaming experiences and social meanings. In: DiGRA 2011 - Proceedings of the 2011 DiGRA International Conference: Think Design Play. DiGRA/Utrecht School of the Arts, January 2011. http://www.digra.org/wp-content/uploads/digital-library/11310.20247.pdf
12. Hilbe, C., Wu, B., Traulsen, A., Nowak, M.A.: Cooperation and control in multiplayer social dilemmas. Proc. Natl. Acad. Sci. **111**(46), 16425–16430 (2014). https://doi.org/10.1073/pnas.1407887111, https://www.pnas.org/content/111/46/16425
13. Kitayama, O.: The wounded caretaker and guilt. Int. Rev. Psych. Anal. **18**, 229–240 (1991)
14. Kurman, J.: Self-enhancement, self-regulation and self-improvement following failures. Br. J. Soc. Psychol. **45**(2), 339–356 (2006)
15. Lee, J.: Climate change games as tools for education and engagement. Nat. Clim. Change. **5**, 413–418 (2015). https://doi.org/10.1038/NCLIMATE2566

16. McClintock, C.G., McNeel, S.P.: Reward and score feedback as determinants of cooperative and competitive game behavior. J. Pers. Soc. Psychol. **4**(6), 606 (1966)
17. Medler, B.: Player dossiers: analyzing gameplay data as a reward. Game. Stud. **11**(1), 1–9 (2011)
18. O'Mara, E.M., Gaertner, L.: Does self-enhancement facilitate task performance? J. Exp. Psychol. Gen. **146**(3), 442 (2017)
19. Ouariachi, T., Olvera-Lobo, M.D., Gutiérrez-Pérez, J., Maibach, E.: A framework for climate change engagement through video games. Environ. Educ. Res. **25**(5), 701–716 (2019). https://doi.org/10.1080/13504622.2018.1545156
20. Parks, C.D., Vu, A.D.: Social dilemma behavior of individuals from highly individualist and collectivist cultures. J. Conflict Resolut. **38**(4), 708–718 (1994). https://doi.org/10.1177/0022002794038004006
21. Richter, G., Raban, D.R., Rafaeli, S.: Studying gamification: the effect of rewards and incentives on motivation. In: Reiners, T., Wood, L.C. (eds.) Gamification in Education and Business, pp. 21–46. Springer, Cham (2015). https://doi.org/10.1007/978-3-319-10208-5_2
22. Rosen, J., Haaga, D.A.F.: Facilitating cooperation in a social dilemma: a persuasion approach. J. Psychol. **132**(2), 143–153 (1998). https://doi.org/10.1080/00223989809599155
23. Ryan, R.M., Deci, E.L.: Self-determination theory and the facilitation of intrinsic motivation, social development, and well-being. Am. Psychol. **55**(1), 68–78 (2000)
24. Schuller, B.W., Dunwell, I., Weninger, F., Paletta, L.: Serious gaming for behavior change: the state of play. IEEE Pervas. Comput. **12**(3), 48–55 (2013). https://doi.org/10.1109/MPRV.2013.54
25. Sedikides, C., Hepper, E.G.: Self-improvement. social and personality psychology. Compass **3**(6), 899–917 (2009)
26. Seelig, B.J., Rosof, L.S.: Normal and pathological altruism. J. Am. Psychoanal. Assoc. **49**(3), 933–959 (2001). https://doi.org/10.1177/00030651010490031901. pMID:11678244
27. Tanenbaum, J.G., Antle, A.N., Robinson, J.: Three perspectives on behavior change for serious games. In: Proceedings of the SIGCHI Conference on Human Factors in Computing Systems, pp. 3389–3392. CHI 2013, Association for Computing Machinery, New York, NY, USA (2013). https://doi.org/10.1145/2470654.2466464
28. Vegt, N., Visch, V., Vermeeren, A., Ridder, H.: Player experiences and behaviors in a multiplayer game: designing game rules to change interdependent behavior. Int. J. Ser. Games. **3**, 69–85 (2016). https://doi.org/10.17083/ijsg.v3i4.150

Interviewing a Virtual Suspect: Conversational Game Characters Using Alexa

Gonçalo Baptista[✉], Diogo Rato, and Rui Prada

INESC-ID and Instituto Superior Técnico, Universidade de Lisboa, Lisbon, Portugal
{goncalo.baptista,diogo.rato,rui.prada}@tecnico.ulisboa.pt

Abstract. The video game industry is constantly innovating, with new mediums and ways for players to interact with the game environment. Voice interaction in games is an ever evolving field, especially with advances in Natural Language Processing. In that vein, there has been a increasing number of conversational agents with natural language interaction capabilities deployed into video games. In this paper, we improve the Virtual Suspect game with a natural language interaction using the tools provided by Amazon Alexa. We followed an iterative, user-centered approach when designing the new interaction, collecting feedback and data from three User Studies in order to improve the interaction with the Virtual Suspect. Our findings suggest that the usage of natural language to support the interaction with game characters can improve the player experience.

Keywords: Conversational agents · Voice games · Interactive narrative

1 Introduction

Videogames offer the player an opportunity to be immersed in virtual worlds enriched with fantastic elements and interesting characters. Interacting with these characters allows players to uncover narrative beats while exploring and progressing through the game's story. These interactions are usually supported by dialogue systems that provide the player with a familiar mechanism to engage characters and extract information: Natural Language. However, such systems often display restrictions that conflict with players' expectations and limit their ability to express themselves. Researchers and developers have applied different paradigms to endow Non-Player Characters (NPCs) with conversational capabilities: from dialogue supported by social exchanges [8,9], to parser-based approaches [7,12] and vast authored branching dialogues [11], all are designed on top of a limited set of utterances. Although these interactions might resemble

This work was supported by national funds through Fundação para a Ciência e a Tecnologia (FCT) with reference UIDB/50021/2020.

conversations between social beings, they are restrictive and do not allow players to engage NPCs in a natural and free fashion.

Video games are constantly evolving and, as an interactive medium, they welcome the application of new technologies to support more believable and interesting player experiences. As such, there has been a significant amount of video games relying on Natural Language Understanding to support the interaction between the players and NPCs [6]. The hardware to support such interaction is becoming more accessible and the increasing number of developer-friendly APIs has boosted the number of applications, in particular games, that have verbal behaviour as the core of the interaction.

Among other solutions commercially available, Alexa is a virtual assistant developed by Amazon and released with the Echo smart speaker that allows developers to add new third-party functionalities, called Skills, which include voice-enabled games. Since this technology allows for the easy creation of natural language applications, and has already been proven to work as a platform for voice interactive games, we decided to use it to create a new natural language interaction with the lying agent created by Rato et al. [14].

Rato et al. [14,15] designed a model for a Virtual Suspect - an autonomous agent that was capable of lying, within an interaction in the context of a police interrogation. This model has the potential to be integrated into a video game as an NPC that players have to interrogate. The focus of that work was designing the architecture of the agent and devising the lying algorithm. When it came to testing the agent, the interaction between users and agent was very limited, only allowing for a small pre-defined number of questions, and not fully showcasing the capabilities of the lying model. In their conclusion, the authors posited that a natural language interaction could improve the quality of the interaction with the agent.

The limited interaction with the original Virtual Suspect game is the problem that we are trying to solve. We believe the core of the original work, the Virtual Suspect framework and lying capabilities, has potential to make for a compelling character in a video game environment, but the original work did not go far enough to showcase that potential, and the interaction they created in order to test their work was insufficient.

We will test the hypothesis that a natural language interaction will improve the interaction with the agent, and create an interaction that showcases the capabilities of the original model and shows its potential as a lying NPC in a video game. From investigative games centered around interrogating a suspect to just a side character in a larger narrative, a good lying NPC with a good interaction could be an interesting component to add to a video game, providing players with a rich and unique experience.

This work will focus on the creation of a new natural language interaction with the Virtual Suspect, using Alexa, as a means of showcasing the lying agent's capabilities and potential. We looked at other works with certain similarities to our own, analysed how the Virtual Suspect [14] was designed and developed, and how we can create our new interaction with the Alexa Skills Kit (ASK). We then combined that knowledge to create a Virtual Suspect Skill and followed a user-centered approach to improve the quality of the interaction. Our goal is a natural language interaction that is fluid and provides good User Experience (UX), and showcases the potential of the lying agent model as a video game component.

2   Related Work

We analysed two examples of Virtual Suspects, one developed by Bitan et al. [1] and another by Bruijnes et al. [2]. While the Virtual Suspect developed by Rato et al. [14] was mostly focused on modelling the lying behaviour of the agent, these two works were more focused on modelling the agent's mental and emotional state [1], and different personality characteristics of the agent [2]. Their work was centered around how the agent's answers would differ according to those parameters, with all the different possibilities being pre-programmed, while the Virtual Suspect that we will base ourselves off of allows the agent to come up with its own answers dynamically. Given that their answers were already pre-defined, the Virtual Suspects' behaviour could eventually become predictable with enough interaction, if incorporated into a video game, while our agent could introduce more variance to the experience.

We studied three examples of Conversational Agents in video game-like environments, to see how other authors have tackled these issues. The work by Falk et al. [3] centers around guiding players through an interactive narrative, how to model knowledge representation in an agent's memory, and how to model a player's perception of that knowledge. They developed an agent that players can talk to during an interactive narrative, they can ask questions about the story, and the agent can guide users to important parts of the narrative they might have missed. Kenny and Huyck [5] developed an agent that can talk with the player and understand what the player is talking about through context, using Referring Expressions. Last but not least, we looked at the work of Morris [10] who proposed a model for an agent with shallow models of emotion and personality that would be capable of engaging players in conversation while playing a Cluedo-style game. These three works highlight the potential of conversational agents, such as the Virtual Suspect developed by Rato et al. [14], to be added to video game environments, and to use Natural Language as the interactive medium. Things like modelling context and player's perception of knowledge will be extremely useful to us when creating the Natural Language interaction with the Virtual Suspect.

We also examined some examples in the industry, with companies like Doppio Games developing and releasing voice-first games for platforms like Amazon Alexa and Google Assistant. These games focus their interaction and gameplay loops on voice interaction and Natural Language Processing, to create an interesting and innovative experience. Examples include The Vortex by Doppio Games, Starfinder by Paizo - Alexa Games, and Escape the Room by Stoked Skills LLC. Not only are companies and developers taking advantage of this new paradigm, but even Amazon itself is fostering the development of new applications using the Alexa Prize [13], a competition for creating open-domain social bots. These games and works serve as an example that this sort of interaction in games is viable.

While these works have aspects in common with our own, none is too similar to what we are trying to achieve, so we could not base ourselves too much on any of them and had to come up with a model for our new Virtual Suspect interaction on our own.

3 Virtual Suspect

In order for us to create a new interaction with the Virtual Suspect, we have to obtain a deep understanding of how it was designed and how it works. In "Virtual Suspect - A Lying Virtual Agent" Rato et al. [14] laid out the architecture and functionality of their lying Virtual Suspect.

First, the agent has a memory, its **Knowledge Base**, which contains its story. The agent's story is composed of *events* and *entities*. Entities are the most basic memory fragment and can represent people, locations, objects, time spans. Events represent distinct episodes in the agent's story and they are composed of an Action and several entities, in different roles. For example, *"John stole a chocolate from the store on September 5th at 4:30 pm"* can be an event where *"Steal"* is the Action, and *"John"*, *"chocolate"*, *"store"* and *"September 5th at 4:30 pm"* are all represented by entities. Entities can have different roles in events. In the previous example, those roles were Agent, Theme, Location, and Time, respectively, but you can also have Manner and Reason. These roles indicate the relation between those entities and the Action in that event, *who* was involved, *what* was the target of the action, *where* it happened, *when* it took place, *how* it happened, and *why* it happened. Events and entities exist separately in the **Knowledge Base**, and events reference the entities that were involved in them, this way the same entity can be referenced by (and thus have participated in) several events. Events can also be true or false, where true events are what really happened in the agent's story and false events are the events the agent uses to lie. These can have an incriminatory value from 0 to 100, depending on how incriminatory each event is, in relation to the crime our Virtual Suspect committed.

The interaction between the agent and the user is done through questions and answers. The user asks the agent a question about its story and the agent responds, with either the truth or a lie (as we will see later). These questions are internally represented as *queries* in the agent's system, and they can either be Validation questions (yes or no), or Information Gathering questions (who, where, when, why, etc.). Each query contains a series of conditions which it seeks to validate in order to find an answer. For example, the question *"When did John steal the chocolate?"* is an Information Gathering question that seeks to retrieve the Time entity from an event that matches the conditions *"Agent Equals John"*, *"Action Equals Steal"* and *"Theme Equals Chocolate"*. The **Query Engine** receives this query, tries to find all the events that match those conditions, and returns a *query response*, which in this case contains the value

"September 5th at 4:30 pm". After this step, the Virtual Suspect also contains a **Natural Language Generator** that transforms the query result into a proper English sentence to be returned to the user as its answer.

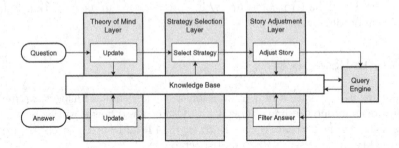

Fig. 1. Virtual Suspect architecture

What enables the agent to lie is a three layered two-pass control system, as illustrated in Fig. 1. When the agent receives a question, it passes through each one of the three layers before being processed by the Query Engine, and the answer passes through the layers again before being returned to the user. The **Theory of Mind Layer** keeps track of what the user already knows about the story, by analysing the information contained inside the query. If the user already knew about John stealing the chocolate, for example, it would not be productive to try to lie about that. The **Strategy Selection Layer** selects an appropriate lying strategy based on the current context, and the **Story Adjustment Layer** creates the fake events that the agent uses in its lies. When the agent encounters a question that would lead it to reveal incriminating information, it instead creates a new fake event with less incriminating information to take the place of the incriminatory event in the version of the story the agent is presenting the user. The agent always keeps track of the true version of events, but is capable of having alternate versions of those events in its memory in order to hide information from the user. After the question has passed through all the layers, it is processed by the Query Engine, and thus the information about the fake events is retrieved instead of the real information, and the result then passes back through the layers again, before being returned to the user.

Figure 2 shows how this was implemented in the original work [14], with the **Response Model** representing the conjunction of the Query Engine and the three layers. The prototype that was originally used to test the Virtual Suspect was a visual interface that contained information about the suspect and the case, and a set number of pre-defined questions that users could select from. All this information, along with the events and entities of the agent's story were all defined in a separate Story file. When the user selected one of the pre-defined questions from the visual interface, it automatically sent the corresponding query to the Response Model, which was then processed as previously described and the answer was displayed back to the user in the interface.

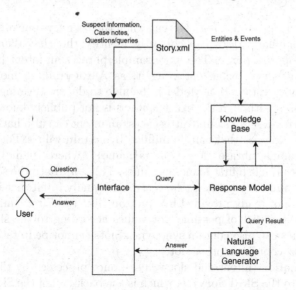

Fig. 2. Virtual suspect prototype implementation

4   Alexa

The Alexa is a virtual assistant developed by Amazon and released with the Echo smart speaker, that is capable of a wide range of features, but the one that is of interest to us is the ability to create third-party applications using the Alexa technology, called Skills. These Skills are made through the Alexa Skills Kit (ASK) and they have two components: the **Interaction Model**, and the **Skill Service**. Figure 3 shows the typical workflow of an Alexa Skill. The user asks a question or gives a command to Alexa, which sends it to the Skill Interaction Model. The Interaction Model disambiguates the meaning of the user's message and sends that information to the Skill Service, which computes the appropriate response and sends it back through the system until it reaches the user.

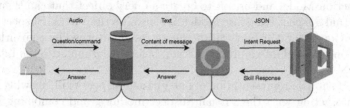

Fig. 3. Workflow of an Alexa Skill

The **Interaction Model** is the front-end of the Skill, and it is composed of *intents*. An intent contains a selection of sample phrases that could be uttered to invoke that intent. For example, a *HelloWorldIntent* could contain the utterances

"Hello", *"Hi World"*, and *"Hey"*, so that when the user says one of these phrases or something similar, Alexa can correctly identify the *HelloWorldIntent* and provide the proper response. The more sample phrases an intent has, the more accurate Alexa can be when detecting it, as Alexa trains a model with the information in our Interaction Model to be able to detect meaning from a wide variety of phrases, although the exact method is not publicly known.

Besides having a set of sample utterances, an intent can also have *slots*, which are essentially variables that can be fulfilled by certain values. For example, we can have the sample phrase *"My name is*{name}*"*, where {name} represents a slot that accepts English first names as values. This way, both the sentences *"My name is John"* and *"My name is Mary"*, would equally fulfill that intent. A slot type can be one of many provided by Amazon (like the First Name slot type), or can be a custom list of possible slot values according to the skill's domain. These slot values can also contain synonyms. Slots cannot be iteratively defined, so a slot cannot contain another slot.

This information (intent and slot values), once processed by the Interaction Model, is sent to the **Skill Service**, which is the back-end of the Skill, through a JSON file. The Skill Service takes the information sent by the Interaction Model and computes the appropriate response (for example, *"Hello John"*), and sends it back to the Interaction Model through another JSON file.

5   Solution

In order to create the new Natural Language interaction with the Virtual Suspect, we combined what we studied in the previous sections to create a Virtual Suspect Skill. Our Interaction Model has different intents for the different question types, and we use slots to create the query conditions. Each of our intents needs lots of sample utterances so our model can cover a wide range of questions, and our slot values include the possible entity values for each type. Our Skill Service was created in the same environment as the original Virtual Suspect was developed, so we can use the original Virtual Suspect Response Model as a sort of code black box. The Skill Service takes the intent and slot information from the Interaction Model and uses it to create a query object that can then be sent to the Virtual Suspect Response Model. We also use the Virtual Suspect Natural Language Generator to transform the query result returned by the Virtual Suspect Response Model into a proper answer, before returning it to the Interaction Model.

Figure 4 shows a representation of our Virtual Suspect Skill, showing the Skill Service interacting with the Virtual Suspect modules, and combining what we had already seen in Figs. 2 and 3. The connection between the Story file and Interaction Model is merely symbolic, as we cannot directly connect those two entities, but it represents the entity values that populate the slot values.

We used an iterative, user-centered approach when designing the Virtual Suspect Skill. We started by recreating the functionality of the original prototype, ensuring basic coverage for all the different types of questions, and then we did

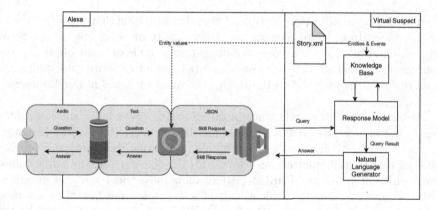

Fig. 4. Solution architecture

a User Study to collect data on how users interacted with the Virtual Suspect, what kinds of questions they wanted to ask and how they asked them. We also measured the performance of the agent, collecting data on the problems of the interaction, so we could have a baseline performance to compare to later.

After we collected the data from the First User Study, we used it to improve upon the interaction, making changes and improvements to fix those issues. We then conducted a Second User Study after those changes, to validate if those changes had improved the quality of the interaction, and to measure the User Experience (UX).

During the development and first two User Studies, we kept the lying component of the agent deactivated, so we could better measure its responses to the various questions without the lies obscuring that information. After we did the Second User Study, we turned the lying component of the agent back on and did a final User Study to measure the UX of that interaction, to see how well the original lying algorithm fit into the new interaction.

The next sections describe the development process of the Virtual Suspect, and the three User Studies, respectively.

6   Development

6.1   First Steps

In order to be able to do our fist User Test and collect data on how people interact with the Virtual Suspect, we needed a functional Virtual Suspect Skill prototype. We started off by replicating the functionality of the original Virtual Suspect Prototype [14] whose visual interface only included 13 pre-defined questions. Since those questions were already predefined and the corresponding queries would directly be sent to the Virtual Suspect Response Model (as seen in Fig. 2), there was no concern about being able to interpret those questions using Natural Language Processing, and as such they did not conform to a consistent style, often having sentences before the question and information that was not relevant for the query. In order to recreate the functionality of being able to ask those original questions (or their corresponding queries at least) and obtaining the same answers, we had to restructure the questions into a more consistent style that we could then expand to the rest of the question types in our Interaction Model.

We ended up with a style where a question like *"Where did you meet John Frey?"* was modeled as *"Where* {question_verb} {subject} {filler_verb} {agent}*"*. In this example, *"Where"* indicates the type of question, {subject} and {agent} are slots that contain information relevant for the query conditions, while {question_verb} and {filler_verb} are slots that allow for a wider range of questions with the same meaning to be identified. This way, questions like *"Did you meet John Frey?"* and *"Have you met John Frey?"* can both be represented by the same utterance, as they both have the same meaning.

After we established a consistent style of question, and managed to recreate the functionality of the original 13 questions, we expanded our Interaction Model to include more questions of each type, by looking at the events of our story and figuring what types of questions could be asked, with which conditions. As we mentioned before, this was done with the lying component turned off, so we could better understand how the agent was processing the information. With a lying agent, it would be more difficult to tell if the agent answered *"No"* because he understood the question and decided to lie, or if he did not understand the question at all.

With this functioning prototype, we realized our First User Study to collect data on how people interacted with the Virtual Suspect, so we could expand our Interaction Model with more possible questions, and to measure the performance of the agent, so we could note the problems with the interaction and work to improve it.

6.2   Improving the Interaction

With the data collected from the First User Study, we were able to make a lot of changes and improvements to the Virtual Suspect Skill, to address problems such as:

- **Missing intents:** questions that the users wanted to ask but the agent was not capable of answering.
- **Pronouns:** both direct pronouns (it, him, there) and indirect pronouns (something, anyone).
- **Context:** a knowledge of what was previously asked.
- **Synonyms:** adding more synonyms to the Interaction Model.
- **Missing information:** information about the story that users wanted to know about but it was not represented in the story.
- **Answer generation:** improving the Virtual Suspect Natural Language Generator.
- **Time conditions:** add more cases for different possible time conditions in questions.

- **More utterances:** add more variety of questions to the Interaction Model.
- **Filters in the Skill Service:** to make sure that things are being processed correctly.
- **Feedback:** providing better feedback to the user when the agent cannot answer a question for some reason.

By addressing these and other problems and making all the necessary changes to the Virtual Suspect Skill, we were able to improve the interaction with the Virtual Suspect. We realized the Second User Study in order to verify that improvement and measure the quality of the interaction.

6.3   Last Adjustments

After we validated the improvements we made with the Second User Study, we made a few final minor adjustments before turning on the lying component again and making sure it was still working as intended with all of our changes. After that, we moved on the Third and final User Study, to test how the lying algorithm was working with the new interaction.

7   User Studies

We conducted three User Studies during the development of our work. In all three studies, users interacted with the Virtual Suspect via a text messaging service, where an account in the name of the Suspect was created to add to user immersion. For all three studies, the conversations between the users and the agent were logged and annotated, in order to identify the problems with the interaction.

Considering that this work is centered around the Alexa, the decision to use text messaging as the means of interacting with the agent might be a strange one, but it was not without reason. Firstly, the global COVID-19 pandemic made it more difficult to organize and conduct user studies, having to do so remotely, which limited our options on how to have users interact with the game. Second, even though Alexa Skills function exactly the same way when interacting via voice or via text, the ability to log the conversations between players and the agent does not, as the Amazon logging services do not save information on the full sentence spoken by the user, only its intent and slots, and as we will see, the ability to thoroughly log the conversations was crucial to our work. Thirdly, and this is not as significant as the other two constraints, our Studies were conducted with non-native English speakers, which could negatively impact the Automatic Speech Recognition capabilities of the Alexa.

For the Second and Third User Studies, a questionnaire was presented to the users after the interaction to measure the User Experience (UX), which used the User Experience Questionnaire (UEQ) developed by Schrepp et al. [16,17].

7.1   First User Study

For the First User Study, we wanted to collect data on how users interacted with the Virtual Suspect (what type of questions they asked, and how they asked those questions) and do an analysis of the problems with the interaction.

Since the interaction was still in an early state and the range of the agent's understanding capabilities was limited, we decided to do two different types of interactions. One where users would interact directly with the Virtual Suspect Skill, and another where users would instead interact with a human pretending to be the Virtual Suspect, answering questions as the Virtual Suspect ideally would without the Skill limitations (following a Wizard-of-Oz technique [4]). This way we could collect data on the problems of the current interaction with the Skill, but also analyse how people would interact without those limitations. When logging the conversations, both types of responses were recorded for either type of interaction, allowing us to do a comparison between what the user actually interacted with and what the other interface would have said instead.

Twelve people participated in this study, none of which had interacted with the Virtual Suspect in any way before. The average number of exchanges per conversation with the Virtual Suspect, across all the participants, was 23.67. The average conversation success rate (which is the percentage of exchanges that were correctly identified by the agent) was 37.29%. We classified problems in two categories: Question Problems (which was anything that caused the question not to be recognized by the agent), and Answer Problems (which was anything that caused the agent to give a bad answer). Only 35.92% of exchanges did not have any Question Problems, while only 22.54% did not have any Answer Problems.

Overall, the results indicate that a more robust Interaction Model was necessary to support a better gameplay experience, as could be expected. Apart from that, we were able to collect valuable insight about how players engage the Virtual Suspect and its capability to reply appropriately, through the use of the aforementioned quantitative annotation of the interactions. This also provided us with a baseline performance with which we could compare future iterations.

7.2   Second User Study

The Second User Study was realized after the changes and improvements made as a result of the data gathered in the First User Study, with the objective of validating those changes, verifying the improvement with the interaction, and measuring the User Experience (UX).

Fourteen people participated in this study, six of which had participated in the First Study and the remaining eight being new participants. This study had an average of 54.07 exchanges per conversation, and an average success rate of 63.39%. This time, 65.13% of exchanges did not have any Question Problems, and 89.83% of exchanges not having any Answer Problems.

These results were a marked improvement over the First Study, validating the changes we made to improve the interaction. Not only that, but the UX results were also very good. Figure 5 shows our results compared to the benchmarks set by the authors of the UEQ [16], and we can see that all of them fall either into the Good or Excellent category.

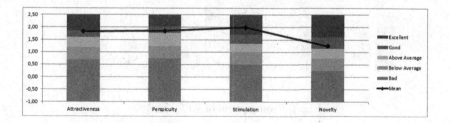

Fig. 5. UEQ benchmarks

This Study was a success, as we were able to definitively show the improvements we made to our Virtual Suspect Skill, validating our previous choices, and we were able to show that our Skill provides a good User Experience.

7.3 Third User Study

The Third User Study was conducted after we turned on the lying component of the Virtual Suspect and its objective was to measure the effect it had on the interaction, to see how well it was working.

This study had sixteen participants, six who had participated in both previous studies, and six who had participated only in the Second, with four new participants. The average number of exchanges per conversation was 46.13, and the success rate was 65.01%. 66.80% of exchanges did not have any Question Problems, and 88.48% did not have any Answer Problems.

The agent performance was largely the same as the Second Study, with the difference in the average number of exchanges being explained by the fact that the interactions of the Second Study were more free and exploratory, while in the Third Study they were more focused on the crimes of the Suspect.

The UEQ results were more telling, with Fig. 6 showing that the results in the Third Study were noticeably worse than the Second Study. Given that the agent performance remained at about the same level, and given the feedback we received about the agent's lies not being very believable or realistic, it is safe to conclude that it was the introduction of the lying component that caused this drop in UX. Therefore, as it stands, the current lying algorithm is not very suited for this new conversational interaction.

8 Discussion

The ongoing development of the Virtual Suspect aligned with the user-centered studies suggests that the employment of a conversational model based on Natural Language can be beneficial to improve the player experience. The user

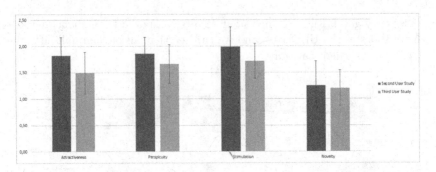

Fig. 6. Comparison of UEQ results

questionnaires further support this claim, since all the evaluated dimensions of the UEQ had positive values. Furthermore, the duration and variety of questions asked during the interaction lead us to believe that introducing such conversational skills affords different interviewing strategies not supported by traditional dialogue systems found in games.

Additionally, regarding the methodology adopted, using a user-centered approach allowed us to better understand the interactive space the players want to and, to an extent, can explore inside the narrative. With each iteration of the Interaction Model, players were able to choose different lines of questioning as well as collect information not accessible before.

However, accommodating conversational intents not widely adopted by the entire sample might introduce a heavy developer and authoring effort, which might not be worthy of consideration. Based on the development of the Virtual Suspect, we realized that the authoring tools provided by Alexa have a restricted set of functionalities that demand a wide variety of sample utterances to generate an adequate interaction model. Constraints like the inability to have slots inside of slots led to an inflation of utterances with the same meaning in the Interaction Model, and kept us from achieving a degree of nuance that would have allowed even more questions to be recognized.

And finally, as we saw in the results of our last User Study, the introduction of the lying mechanism negatively affected the user experience. Although not being the focus of this work, the introduction of new conversational capabilities required some modification to the story representation. The way the lying algorithm was defined in the original work did not adequately accommodate these new story elements and structures. A more nuanced and thorough lying algorithm is needed to better take advantage of and demonstrate the more advanced capabilities and natural interaction of the Virtual Suspect game. Furthermore, during the course of this research, we realized that the development of the Interaction Model should be deeply linked to the querying mechanism that retrieves information. Pursuing a disconnected development of the interaction and the knowledge representation does not benefit the capacity of the agent as a whole and, ultimately, compromising the player experience.

9   Conclusion

The deployment of conversational agents in games should not aim to replace classical dialogue systems but rather explore new gameplay opportunities that are driven by voice interaction as its core mechanic. In this work, we followed a user-centered approach in pursuit of our objective of improving the interaction with the Virtual Suspect, and the deployment of conversational agents in games. We were able to overcome the limitations of the original Virtual Suspect interaction [14], create a Natural Language interaction that showcased the capabilities of the Virtual Suspect, and, most importantly, support conversation with a game character with good UX. On top of achieving our goal of improving the interaction with the Virtual Suspect, we were able to test whether the original lying algorithm [14] was suited to this type of interaction, and concluded that it needs further improvement.

Regarding the Interaction Model structure, the authoring approach can be improved. A different natural language model, something more non-deterministic and grammar-like, could be beneficial in achieving an even better interaction with a reduced authoring effort.

There were also constraints with the definitions of the Virtual Suspect Architecture, like the way that Time and Reason entities were defined within events, that kept us from being able to achieve a more realistic story that would have matched the more natural interaction we created. A restructuring of the agent's memory, keeping the same basic concepts but improving upon them, could lay the foundation for a richer and more realistic story.

The other objective of this work was to showcase the Virtual Suspect capabilities and demonstrate its potential as an addition to a video game environment as a lying NPC. The fact that we were able to create a Natural Language interaction with good UX does seem to support that hypothesis, and the work that we have done so far can easily be expanded upon in the future. However, further research must be conducted.

The future of this work should be centered on either creating an interactive video game centered around interrogating the Virtual Suspect, or incorporating the Virtual Suspect lying model into an already established video game environment. The improvements to the interaction with the agent itself, like the new Natural Language Model, a restructuring of the agent's memory, or a new lying algorithm, can still be considered depending on the needs and context of the eventual work, as well as writing new stories and characters.

References

1. Bitan, M., Nahari, G., Nisin, Z., Roth, A., Kraus, S.: Psychologically based virtual-suspect for interrogative interview training. In: Thirty-First AAAI Conference on Artificial Intelligence (2017)
2. Bruijnes, M., Wapperom, S., op den Akker, R., Heylen, D.: A virtual suspect agent's response model. In: Affective Agents, p. 17 (2014)

3. Falk, J., Poulakos, S., Kapadia, M., Sumner, R.W.: PICA: proactive intelligent conversational agent for interactive narratives. In: Proceedings of the 18th International Conference on Intelligent Virtual Agents, pp. 141–146. ACM (2018)

4. Hajdinjak, M., Mihelic, F.: Conducting the wizard-of-Oz experiment. Informatica (Slovenia) **28**(4), 425–429 (2004)

5. Kenny, I., Huyck, C.: An embodied conversational agent for interactive videogame environments. In: Proceedings of the AISB 2005 Symposium on Conversational Informatics for Supporting Social Intelligence and Interaction, pp. 58–63 (2005)

6. Kiiski, T.: Voice games: the history of voice interaction in digital games (2020)

7. Mateas, M., Stern, A.: Façade: an experiment in building a fully-realized interactive drama. In: Game Developers Conference, vol. 2, pp. 4–8 (2003)

8. McCoy, J., Treanor, M., Samuel, B., Reed, A.A., Wardrip-Fruin, N., Mateas, M.: Prom week. In: Proceedings of the International Conference on the Foundations of Digital Games, pp. 235–237 (2012)

9. McCoy, J., Treanor, M., Samuel, B., Wardrip-Fruin, N., Mateas, M.: Comme il Faut: a system for authoring playable social models. In: Seventh Artificial Intelligence and Interactive Digital Entertainment Conference. Citeseer (2011)

10. Morris, T.W.: Conversational agents for game-like virtual environments. In: AAAI 2002 Spring Symposium on Artificial Intelligence and Interactive Entertainment, pp. 82–86 (2002)

11. Obsidian Entertainment: The outer worlds. [Windows, Playstation 4, Xbox One] (2019)

12. Ocelot Society: Event[0]. [PC Digital] (2016)

13. Ram, A., et al.: Conversational AI: the science behind the Alexa prize. arXiv preprint arXiv:1801.03604 (2018)

14. Rato, D., Prada, R., Paiva, A.: Virtual Suspect. Master's thesis, Instituto Superior Técnico, October 2016

15. Rato, D., Ravenet, B., Prada, R., Paiva, A.: Strategically misleading the user: building a deceptive virtual suspect. In: Proceedings of the 16th Conference on Autonomous Agents and MultiAgent Systems, pp. 1711–1713. International Foundation for Autonomous Agents and Multiagent Systems (2017)

16. Schrepp, M.: User Experience Questionnaire Handbook. All You Need to Know to Apply the UEQ Successfully in Your Project (2015)

17. Schrepp, M., Hinderks, A., Thomaschewski, J.: User experience questionnaire. Mensch und Computer 2017-Tagungsband: Spielend einfach interagieren **17**, 355 (2018)

SimpAI: Evolutionary Heuristics for the ColorShapeLinks Board Game Competition

Pedro M. A. Fernandes[1] , Pedro M. A. Inácio[1] , Hugo Feliciano[1] ,
and Nuno Fachada[1,2(✉)]

[1] School of Communication, Arts and Information Technologies, Lusófona University,
Lisbon, Portugal
{a21803791,a21802050,a21805809}@alunos.ulht.pt,
nuno.fachada@ulusofona.pt
[2] COPELABS, Lusófona University, Lisbon, Portugal

Abstract. We present SimpAI, an AI agent created for the *ColorShapeLinks* competition, based on an arbitrarily sized version of the Simplexity board game. The agent uses a highly efficient parallelized Minimax-type search, with an heuristic function composed of several partial heuristics, the balance of which was optimized with an evolutionary algorithm. SimpAI was the runner-up in the competition's most challenging session, which required an AI agent with good adaptation capabilities.

Keywords: Board games · Artificial intelligence · Evolutionary heuristics · Simplexity · ColorShapeLinks

1 Introduction

In this paper, we present SimpAI, an artificial intelligence (AI) agent created for the *ColorShapeLinks* board game competition [3]. This competition is based on an arbitrarily sized version of the Simplexity board game [1]. In this game, the board is a vertically placed grid and pieces fall with gravity. In a similar fashion to Connect-4, the first player to place n pieces of the same type in a sequence, wins. Pieces are defined by color, white or red, and shape, round or square. The first player wins with round or white pieces, while the second player wins with square or red pieces. Shape has priority over color as a winning condition, and while players only play with pieces of their color, they can play with pieces of both shapes, making the game more interesting and complex.

In a standard Simplexity game, the board has six rows and seven columns, and victory can be achieved with a sequence of four pieces of the same shape or color, either vertically, horizontally or diagonally. Figure 1 shows the possible victory conditions for both players in a standard Simplexity game, i.e., either by color or by shape, with the latter having priority as shown in Fig. 1b and Fig. 1d.

P. M. A. Fernandes and P. M. A. Inácio—These authors contributed equally to this work.

© Springer Nature Switzerland AG 2022
I. Barbedo et al. (Eds.): VJ 2020, CCIS 1531, pp. 113–126, 2022.
https://doi.org/10.1007/978-3-030-95305-8_9

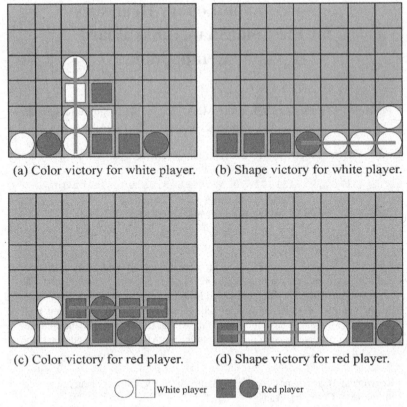

(a) Color victory for white player.   (b) Shape victory for white player.

(c) Color victory for red player.   (d) Shape victory for red player.

⬭☐ White player   ■● Red player

Fig. 1. Victory conditions for the Simplexity board game.

The SimpAI agent was developed as a learning and exploration project in the context of an AI course unit at Lusófona University's Bachelor in Videogames degree [4]. It searches for the best solutions in the game board using a classical Minimax-type search approach, with a number of optimizations to search as deep and wide as possible. The search is guided by a composition of five heuristics, the weights of which were optimized using an evolutionary algorithm. The agent finished the competition in second place in the *Unknown Track*, for which the board configuration and time to play were only announced after the competition deadline.

This paper is organized as follows. In Sect. 2, we review board game AI techniques, as well as two competing agents in the first edition of the *ColorShapeLinks* competition. In Sect. 3, we discuss in detail the proposed agent, namely the optimized search algorithm, the implemented heuristics and how we performed heuristic weight optimization using evolutionary algorithms. In Sect. 4 we describe the results obtained using this approach and how the agent fared in the two competition tracks. A discussion of these results takes place in Sect. 5. Section 6 closes the paper, discussing potential improvements and offering some conclusions.

2 Background

The classical search approach in board game AI is the Minimax algorithm [8, 11]. This algorithm performs a depth-first search of the game tree down to a predefined search depth, bubbling up board evaluations obtained at maximum depth with a given heuristic function in a recursive fashion. Minimax evaluates game states at each depth from the AI's perspective, while assuming the adversary will also choose the best move for himself. As such, Minimax *maximizes* board evaluations when the AI is playing, *minimizing* them in the opponent's turn. Minimax has been optimized and improved through the years. Some of these optimizations, discussed for example in reference [8], are summarized in the following paragraphs.

Negamax is one of the most basic improvements to Minimax, evaluating boards from the perspective of who is playing at a given depth. The code ends up being simpler and slightly more efficient than a pure Minimax, since the algorithm only performs maximizations. Conversely, Alpha-beta pruning is a crucial optimization for Minimax (or Negamax), making use of the upper and lower bound evaluations returned by the heuristic function – the search window – in order to determine if a branch from a specific move is worth exploring further, pruning it in case its evaluation crosses these limits.

Aspiration search takes this idea further, attempting to narrow the search window in order to prune more branches, speeding up the algorithm. It accomplishes this by calling the algorithm with a range based on the previous search, the lower bound being the subtraction of a window size to the previous result and the upper bound being the addition of the window size to the previous result.

The Negascout optimization performs a scout test by fully examining the first move of each board position with a wide search window, using the resulting score to narrow the search window for the following moves. If all these following moves fail, the algorithm conducts the search again with a full width search window. From the initial move with a wide search window, the algorithm derives an approximation for the window sizes for successive moves, while also pruning large numbers of branches.

Move ordering works in tandem with Alpha-Beta pruning, ordering the possible moves at each depth by their heuristic score, from highest to lowest, so the algorithm evaluates the most likely best moves first, increasing the chances of pruning potentially worse branches and therefore making the algorithm perform faster and explore further.

Iterative deepening is an optimization which works well with a time limit. It searches with incremental depths, and keeps going while it still has time to keep searching. It essentially performs depth-first search in a breadth-first fashion, allowing the AI to use as much time as it can without going over a preestablished time limit.

Zobrist hashing makes use of an hash table and a collective of various integer numbers for each position of the board, all different, that are later used by the AI to convert a given board state into a rapidly storable and retrievable numerical identifier. These values are stored in a hash table along with the heuristic score for the respective board states, thus avoiding heuristic reevaluation of the latter.

The state of the art in board game AI can be considered a combination of Monte Carlo Tree Search (MCTS) and deep reinforcement learning [6, 8, 11]. MCTS works by simulating as many random play outs as possible from a given board state while there is available thinking time, selecting a move based on the amount of wins, ties and losses for each node. In turn, deep reinforcement learning combines artificial neural networks with reinforcement learning (e.g., QLearning), enabling the AI to learn the best possible moves in any given board state.

Concerning the first edition of the *ColorShapeLinks* competition, the winners of each track used a number of techniques discussed in the previous paragraphs. The ThunderAI agent won the *Base Track* using MCTS with a custom board implementation. In turn, the first place in the *Unknown Track* was claimed by SureAI, a very well tuned Negamax-based agent.

3 Methods

The SimpAI agent was developed in C# (.NET Standard 2.0 [10]), a requirement for the competition as the agents need to run both in the Unity game engine [9] and in the console. The implementation is divided into two different parts, which work together to form SimpAI:

1. The search algorithm, used to search for promising future moves in the time it has available to think, discussed in Subsect. 3.1.
2. The heuristic, used to classify future board states according to their strategic value, thus guiding the search algorithm towards finding the best move. The heuristic is presented in Subsect. 3.2.

In practice, the heuristic is a combination of several partial heuristics. These are weighted in order to give the final heuristic value for each board state. The optimized weights were obtained using an evolutionary algorithm, as discussed in Subsect. 3.3.

3.1 Search

The search is conducted through a Negamax algorithm, with a number of optimizations, namely alpha-beta pruning, move ordering, iterative deepening and zobrist hashing, all of which were discussed in Sect. 2.

The search was also parallelized, allowing several branches to be evaluated at the same time by distributing the workload by the available CPU cores. In practice, this was achieved with the `Parallel.Invoke()` method in C#, which internally optimizes the number of available worker threads according to the number of hardware threads. Since the Minimax family of search algorithms works recursively, and recursive algorithms are difficult to parallelize effectively [2], each possible move at the first depth level is processed iteratively in the main thread. Then, each corresponding Minimax (Negamax) subtree, from the second depth level and onwards, is recursively processed in one of the available worker threads, as shown in Fig. 2. When all the threads finish their work, results for each subtree are compared back in the main thread, and the branch with the best heuristic score determines the move to perform.

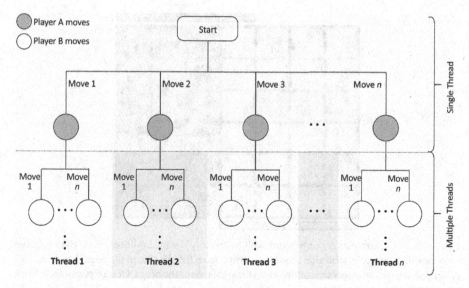

Fig. 2. Parallelization strategy for SimpAI. The first level of depth is iteratively processed in a single thread. From level 2 onwards, each subtree is recursively processed in one of m available threads. For simplification, it is assumed that there are always n moves to be performed at each depth level. Player A represents the player about to play and Player B the player that plays afterwards.

3.2 Heuristics

The heuristic value for each board state is determined by the weighted sum of five partial heuristics, discussed in the following paragraphs.

HorizCenterHeuristic considers the overlapping area between a winning sequence starting from the left side of the board with another from the right side as a more valuable location for a player's piece. Pieces included in this overlapping area, shown in orange in Fig. 3 for a board with Simplexity's standard dimensions, are able to be a part of a sequence expanding to their right and another expanding to their left. Positions outside this interval are too close to the edge of the board to allow such sequences; therefore, as their distance to the overlap interval increases, the less valuable these positions become according to *HorizCenterHeuristic*.

VertCenterHeuristic is the vertical counterpart of *HorizCenterHeuristic*, as shown in Fig. 4.

VertDiscHeuristic considers the area above the number of rows needed to form a vertical winning sequence starting at the bottom of the board as a poor location to place pieces. As shown in Fig. 5, positions above this threshold, displayed in grey, are largely out of reach in an early game, with a winning sequence containing these top spaces requiring a large amount of pieces below them. These are only likely to be part of the winning sequence if the game reaches a very advanced stage where only this area is available.

BuildFromAfarHeuristic considers that placing pieces far away from each other while still at a distance that would allow for a winning sequence between them is a

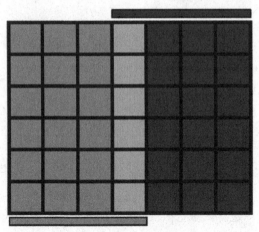

Fig. 3. *HorizCenterHeuristic* on a board with Simplexity's standard dimensions. Blue columns show positions where a horizontal sequence starting from the left side of the board can form. Red columns likewise for sequences starting from the right side of the board. Orange positions indicate where these sequences overlap.

valuable move. In the sequence portrayed in Fig. 6, an agent following this heuristic – first to play – places a piece in the center of the board. Once the adversary places its first piece, the agent answers with a piece in a position at a distance equal to a winning sequence and with an open path to the piece in the middle. If the adversary blocks this potential sequence, the agent places a piece in the opposite position at a winning sequence distance from the center piece. Eventually, the adversary has his pieces nullified (with no way of making an horizontal winning sequence) and the agent has two possible winning sequences.

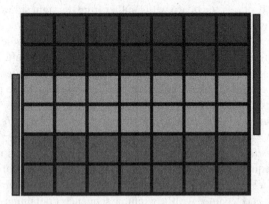

Fig. 4. *VertCenterHeuristic* on a board with Simplexity's standard dimensions. Blue lines show positions where a vertical sequence starting from the bottom of the board can form. Red lines likewise for sequences starting from the top. Orange positions indicate where these sequences overlap.

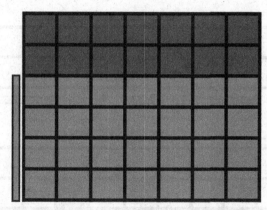

Fig. 5. *VertDiscHeuristic* on a board with Simplexity's standard dimensions. Blue rows can be used to form a vertical winning sequence starting from the bottom of the board. Grey positions are outside this interval.

By placing pieces far from each other while at the same time putting them at a distance that allows for a winning sequence, enables the agent to possibly – according to the board's length – start three different horizontal sequences: i) left to the leftmost piece, ii) between both placed pieces, or, iii) to the right of the rightmost piece. This pressures the adversary to decide which possible sequence to preemptively stop, with this heuristic allowing for the agent to immediately continue another sequence that may, once again, force a similar decision on the adversary, changing its focus from building its sequences to trying to stop the agent's ones.

DumpFromAfarHeuristic takes into account that placing the adversary's shape pieces in the corner of the map is the safest way of neutralizing them, as these are the easiest positions to isolate, as shown in Fig. 7.

Any winning sequence will require at least one space from the areas calculated by *HorizCenterHeuristic* and/or *VertCenterHeuristic*. Therefore, spaces lose value according to how far they are from these intervals. Taking this into account, *DumpFromAfarHeuristic* defines these lower value spaces as ideal locations to dispose of adversarial pieces.

3.3 Heuristic Weight Optimization with Evolutionary Algorithms

The weights of each partial heuristic were obtained with an evolutionary algorithm implemented with the DEAP library [5]. The algorithm population is composed of n individuals representing SimpAI agent instances, with various partial heuristic weights. Each individual is defined by five attributes corresponding to the heuristic weights, as shown in Fig. 8.

Individuals in the first generation are initialized with random weights. The fitness of individuals in each generation is given by their score in a *ColorShapeLinks* competition between them. In this competition, all individuals play against all others, and all have the opportunity to play first against any given opponent.

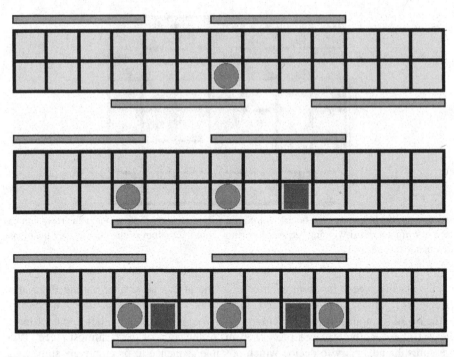

Fig. 6. Three stages (progressing from top to bottom) of an agent using *BuildFromAfarHeuristic* to make decisions on the bottom horizontal slice of a board with 13 columns and a winning sequence of 4 pieces. The orange bars indicate the relevant winning sequences. The agent's pieces appear in blue, while the adversary's appear in red. Both use their specific piece shapes in this example.

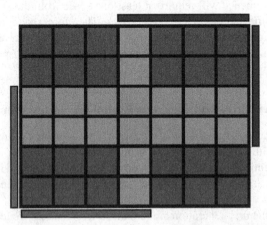

Fig. 7. *DumpFromAfarHeuristic* on a board with Simplexity's standard dimensions. Orange spaces indicate the areas that are part of the *HorizCenterHeuristic* or *VertCenterHeuristic* valuable areas. Grey positions are outside these intervals.

Individual				
HorizCenterHeuristic weight	VertCenterHeuristic weight	VertDiscHeuristic weight	BuiltFromAfarHeuristic weight	DumpFromAfarHeuristic weight

Fig. 8. An individual in the evolutionary algorithm population is defined by five attributes corresponding to the weights of the partial heuristics.

Individuals are selected for the next generation using tournament selection [7], completely replacing the original population. In tournament selection, two individuals are randomly drawn from the original population. A copy of the one with best fitness is selected for the next generation, and then both individuals are returned to the original population and can be selected again. This process is repeated n times, yielding the base population for the new generation.

Each pair of individuals in this new base population then undergoes uniform crossover with probability p_c, being replaced in place by their offspring. Uniform crossover means that each attribute between the mating individuals is swapped with probability p_{c_a}.

Mutation is the final step in defining the new generation of individuals. Individuals undergo mutation with probability p_m, and in these, mutation is applied to each attribute with probability p_{m_a}. Since attributes – i.e. the heuristic weights – are numeric, a gaussian mutation operator, in which a value drawn from the normal distribution (mean μ, standard deviation σ) is added to an attribute, is the most natural choice.

At this point a new generation of n individuals is fully formed. Their fitness is then obtained by performing a new *ColorShapeLinks* competition between them, similar to what was done for the first generation. The algorithm stops when it reaches a predefined number of iterations, l, returning the individuals ordered by fitness, from best to worst. Otherwise the process starts over, with a new generation undergoing selection, crossover and mutation, further improving the heuristic weights of the population.

4   Results

4.1   Heuristic Weight Optimization

After testing several parameter combinations for the evolutionary algorithms, we settled for the values displayed in Table 1. These values provided a good balance between optimization quality and the duration of the optimization process – which was performed using standard Simplexity rules.

We performed five runs of the evolutionary algorithm with different initial populations, and the best individual at the end of each run was selected for a final competition. The final standings for this competition, as well as the weights of each of these "best" individuals, are presented in Table 2.

Naturally, the individual in the first position was selected as our final agent for the *ColorShapeLinks* competition.

Table 1. Parameters used for the evolutionary algorithm runs.

Param.	Value	Description
n	50	Population size
l	500	Number of generations
p_c	0.4	Crossover probability for pairs of individuals
p_{c_a}	0.5	Crossover probability for each attribute
p_m	0.2	Mutation probability per individual
p_{m_a}	0.5	Mutation probability for each attribute
μ	0.0	Mean of normal distribution used for mutation
σ	0.25	Standard deviation of normal distribution used for mutation

Table 2. Weights of the partial heuristics for the best individuals in five runs of the evolutionary algorithm. Position (Pos.) refers to the position of the individual in a final competition between these individuals.

Heuristic	Pos.				
	1st	2nd	3rd	4th	5th
HorizCenter	0.5386	0.8322	1.0383	0.9882	0.7913
VertCenter	4.5551	8.0820	0.1755	6.9733	5.4766
VertDisc	−0.9044	−0.5215	8.4260	0.2584	0.0797
BuildFromAfar	2.9906	2.2055	3.4491	2.3593	5.5618
DumpFromAfar	4.9090	6.7064	3.3461	6.7073	4.1143

4.2 The *ColorShapeLinks* Competition

The competition was held on two tracks, each having specific parameter values, and naturally, separate final standings. The first session, the *Base Track*, was run on Simplexity's default board configuration, as shown in Table 3. Here, agents were limited to one CPU core.

The second session, the *Unknown Track*, was held in a configuration to be defined by the results of that week's EuroMillions draw, after the final submission deadline. This way, the AI agents were unable to specifically prepare for this configuration. The final parameters for this session are also shown in Table 3. There were no limits in the access to the CPU cores, with the AIs being able to take full advantage of the available computing power, provided multithreading was implemented.

In the *Base Track*, the submitted AI was ranked 6th – the last position, thus a clearly poor result. On the other hand, in the *Unknown Track*, SimpAI, working at its full multithreaded capacity, was the runner-up, proving that it can be efficient and adapt to boards of different dimensions.

5 Discussion

5.1 Optimization of Heuristic Weights

By analyzing the five individuals from Table 2, it is possible to notice some patterns, with only the individual in the 3rd position clearly deviating from the rest. All individuals, except the 3rd and 5th, had both *VertCenter* and *DumpFromAfar* heuristics with relatively high values, suggesting the expected synergy between the two. Another similarity between the individuals, except with the 3rd, was the fact they all considered the *HorizCenterHeuristic* less effective than its vertical counterpart.

Table 3. Configurations for the two competition tracks.

Parameter	Value	
	Base Track	*Unknown Track*
Rows	6	8
Columns	7	13
Win Sequence	4	4
Round Pieces	10	26
Square Pieces	11	26
Time limit (ms)	200	325

Considering how the 3rd individual contrasts with the rest of the group, it is important to try and find a difference between the agents classified above and below it, possibly giving further insight as to how the heuristics may have influenced the tournament results. The most significant difference between the two groups has to do with the *VertDiscHeuristic*: the top 2 individuals have a negative value, while the 4th and 5th do not. This means that the 3rd individual specifically defeated agents with positive *VertDiscHeuristic* weight and that, unlike it, considered *VertCenterHeuristic* more valuable than *HorizCenterHeuristic*. This tells us that matches between them may have extended to the higher spaces of the board and, due to a conflict between *VertDiscHeuristic* and *HorizCenterHeuristic*, the 4th and 5th individuals did not try to get the spaces where the areas of both heuristics overlapped, with the 3rd agent capturing them and gaining control of that area of the board, significantly increasing its chances of victory.

As already stated, all individuals, except the 3rd, valued *VertCenterHeuristic* quite more than *HorizCenterHeuristic*. We argue several possible reasons, which individually or in combination, may have led to this outcome:

1. Simplexity's standard dimensions – used for the tournaments ran by the evolutionary algorithm – have more columns than rows. This may have affected the *HorizCenterHeuristic* performance, as it would be triggered less often and more games would have been won due to *VertCenterHeuristic*, since there would not be as many played positions in its *HorizCenter* area.

2. *VertCenterHeuristic* is more efficient than the horizontal version. Regardless of the size of their central areas, *VertCenterHeuristic*'s central area is more accessible due to being in a location very likely to be reached in most games: the middle rows of the board. Contrary to this, *HorizCenterHeuristic*'s central area extends to the top of the board, and consequently, an AI prioritizing this heuristic may be wasting its pieces in positions not as commonly reached in an average game.

3. The *HorizCenterHeuristic*'s weight may have been affected by a conflict with *VertDiscHeuristic*. This is further explored below when analyzing the latter's weight.

In any case, the optimization process clearly led to agents which "understood" the importance of both *CenterHeuristics*, recognizing their overlaying areas as the most valuable board positions.

The most unexpected weight was that of *VertDiscHeuristic*, with it having been attributed a negative value for the top 2 contenders. We highlight two possibilities as to why this may have happened:

1. The heuristic only has real influence in the agent's decision if it is choosing a play in a board where there are available positions in and out of its top area. In other words, there may be several games where *VertDiscHeuristic* is never actually used, for example when the area immediately below it is sufficient to finish games before *VertDiscHeuristic* is actually employable. The top 2 individuals may have won most of their games by mostly following the other heuristics.

2. The fact that *VertDiscHeuristic* weights are negative in the top 2 individuals may be a coincidence related with the initial randomization of weights in the optimization process. However, there may be an actual reason as to why these weights are negative, and we argue it may be related with a conflict between *VertDiscHeuristic* and *HorizCenterHeuristic*. The latter's center area consists of columns that extend to the top of the board, meaning that part of them will come in conflict with the former's "exclusion" zone. It may be that, by affecting the value of the overlapping positions of both heuristics' area of influence, *VertDiscHeuristic* deters the agent from taking top center spaces, leaving them open for the opponent to take, possibly costing games that extended to the final stages. This would mean that *VertDiscHeuristic* ended up doing more harm than good, and by negatively weighting it, the optimization process recognized those top center positions as important for the late-game.

Summing up, it is possible to identify the best combination as having *VertCenter-Heuristic* and *DumpFromAfarHeuristic* as the most valuable, working together to get rid of and isolate the opponent's pieces, while at the same time maintaining overall control of the board; and *VertDiscHeuristic* with a negative weight, so that it does not conflict with *HorizCenterHeurtistic*.

5.2 Performance of SimpAI in the *ColorShapeLinks* Competition

In retrospective, the poor result of SimpAI in the *Base Track* can most likely be attributed to the track's technical restrictions, which limited computing power to one CPU processor. SimpAI, designed from the ground up for using multiple processors, did not scale well under these restrictions. Furthermore, even with the use of Zobrist hashing, having five, completely separate partial heuristics – instead of a faster, single one – probably took its toll when evaluating boards. As such, it is our belief that part of this result stems from the fact that SimpAI was not able to search as deep as its opponents, in spite of the implemented optimizations.

The *Unknown Track* took place on a workstation with 8 cores/16 threads[1]. This was most likely the reason that, SimpAI, working at its full capacity, finished second – thus offsetting the computational weight of using five separate heuristics.

6 Conclusions and Future Work

In this paper we presented SimpAI, an AI agent created for the *ColorShapeLinks* board game competition. The agent was implemented with an efficient Minimax-type search, and an heuristic function composed of five different partial heuristics, the weights of which were optimized with an evolutionary algorithm. SimpAI reached the second position in the *Unknown Track*, a promising result given the fact that the track's parameters were unknown beforehand, thus requiring an AI agent with good adaptation capabilities.

There are some elements that are likely to bring significant improvements to the agent's performance. For example, a wider initial set of partial heuristics could help refine what are indeed the most important features for winning *ColorShapeLinks* matches. From the results, it was clear that some heuristics, such as *VertDiscHeuristic*, did not work out as we initially envisioned – and could probably be excluded altogether, speeding up board evaluations. Additionally, a few partial heuristics use "magic" numbers to provide their evaluation. These could also be considered as parameters to be optimized by the evolutionary algorithm, further refining a winning strategy. Regarding the optimization process, a more comprehensive experimentation with the evolutionary operators and their parameterization could potentially yield better winning combinations. Finally, and while this was not the intended learning goal for the authors of this project, the use of MCTS, deep learning and/or reinforcement learning, could potentially produce stronger and harder to beat agents.

Acknowledgements. This work was supported by Fundação para a Ciência e a Tecnologia under Grant No.: UIDB/04111/2020 (COPELABS).

References

1. Brain Bender Games: Simplexity. Discovery Bay Games (2009). https://boardgamegeek.com/boardgame/55810/simplexity
2. Eliahu, D., Spillinger, O., Fox, A., Demmel, J.: FRPA: A Framework for Recursive Parallel Algorithms. Master's thesis, EECS Department, University of California, Berkeley, May 2015. http://www2.eecs.berkeley.edu/Pubs/TechRpts/2015/EECS-2015-28.html
3. Fachada, N.: ColorShapeLinks: A board game AI competition for educators and students. Comput. Educ.: Artif. Intell. **2**, 100014 (2021). https://doi.org/10.1016/j.caeai.2021.100014

---

[1] Information provided by the organizers at our request.

4. Fachada, N., Códices, N.: Top-down design of a CS curriculum for a computer games BA. In: Proceedings of the 2020 ACM Conference on Innovation and Technology in Computer Science Education, ITiCSE 2020, pp. 300–306. ACM, New York, June 2020. https://doi.org/10.1145/3341525.3387378

5. Fortin, F.A., De Rainville, F.M., Gardner, M.A., Parizeau, M., Gagné, C.: DEAP: evolutionary algorithms made easy. J. Mach. Learn. Res. **13**, 2171–2175 (2012)

6. François-Lavet, V., Henderson, P., Islam, R., Bellemare, M.G., Pineau, J.: An introduction to deep reinforcement learning. Found. Trends® Mach. Learn. **11**(3–4), 219–354 (2018). https://doi.org/10.1561/2200000071

7. Goldberg, D.E., Deb, K.: A comparative analysis of selection schemes used in genetic algorithms. In: Rawlins, G.J. (ed.) Foundations of Genetic Algorithms, vol. 1, pp. 69–93. Elsevier, Amsterdam (1991). https://doi.org/10.1016/B978-0-08-050684-5.50008-2

8. Millington, I.: AI for Games, 3rd edn. CRC Press, Boca Raton (2019). https://doi.org/10.1201/9781351053303

9. Unity Technologies: Unity® (2020). https://unity.com/

10. Wenzel, M., et al.: .NET Standard. Microsoft Docs, March 2020. https://docs.microsoft.com/dotnet/standard/net-standard

11. Yannakakis, G.N., Togelius, J.: Artificial Intelligence and Games. Springer, Cham (2018). https://doi.org/10.1007/978-3-319-63519-4. http://gameaibook.org

Reinforcement Learning in Tower Defense

Augusto Dias[1], Juliano Foleiss[1], and Rui Pedro Lopes[2(✉)] (iD)

[1] Universidade Técnica Federal do Paraná, Curitiba, Brazil
[2] Research Center in Digitalization and Industrial Robotics,
Instituto Politécnico de Bragança, Bragança, Portugal
`rlopes@ipb.pt`

Abstract. Reinforcement learning is a machine learning technique that makes a decision based on a sequence of actions. This allows changing a game agent's behavior through feedback, such as rewards or penalties for their actions. Recent work has been demonstrating the use of reinforcement learning to train agents capable of playing electronic games and obtain scores even higher than professional human players. These intelligent agents can also assume other roles, such as creating more complex challenges to players, improving the ambiance of more complex interactive games and even testing the behavior of players when the game is in development. Some literature has been using a deep learning technique to process an image of the game. This is known as the deep Q network and is used to create an intermediate representation and then process it by layers of neural network. These layers are capable of mapping game situations into actions that aim to maximize a reward over time. However, this method is not feasible in modern games, rendered in high resolution with an increasing frame rate. In addition, this method does not work for training agents who are not shown on the screen. In this work we propose a reinforcement learning pipeline based on neural networks, whose input is metadata, selected directly in the game state, and the actions are mapped directly into high-level actions by the agent. We propose this architecture for a tower defense player agent, a real time strategy game whose agent is not represented on the screen directly.

Keywords: Reinforcement learning · Artificial intelligence · Neural network · Tower Defense

1 Introduction

One of the main goals of the Artificial Intelligence (AI) field is to produce fully autonomous agents that interact with their environments to learn optimal behaviors, improving over time through trial and error. Creating AI systems that are responsive and can effectively learn has been a long-standing challenge, from robots, which can perceive and react to the environment around them, to purely software-based agents, who can interact with natural language and multimedia [12].

Within the AI field of study there are various approaches, proposed models and architectures. Supervised machine learning is an approach in which the training process

I. Barbedo et al. (Eds.): VJ 2020, CCIS 1531, pp. 127–139, 2022.
https://doi.org/10.1007/978-3-030-95305-8_10

is based on previously annotated training set. The process requires that the agent maps the input with the output, adjusting in accordance to the obtained error. However, in a situation where there is a very large sequence of actions to be labeled, this approach becomes unfeasible.

Another approach is Reinforcement Learning (RL), which can be determined as a mathematical structure based on psychological and neurological principles for autonomous experience-oriented learning. In this situation, labeled input/output pairs are not needed. The network learns by exploiting previous knowledge (through a reward mathematical function) to make decisions in new situations. These have been assuming an important role in many situations, particularly in video games.

Talking about video games, intelligent agents can create more challenging situations for the player. In particular, the elaboration of strategies according to the player's behavior in the environment can make the actions of the autonomous agents cease to be obvious and predictable.

An interesting category of video games include strategy games and, in particular, of the Tower Defense (TD) genre. This type of game requires strategic thinking over time to formulate a plan that maximizes the player's survival time. As it is impractical to label the actions that the agent must take at each moment of time, reinforcement learning is a viable learning strategy for the problem.

1.1 Tower Defense

Real-time Strategy (RTS) are games in which the player manages several characters or units with the objective of prevailing in some kind of conflict or obtaining some specific achievement [1]. In general, this challenge is significantly more difficult than the planning challenge in classic board games, such as chess, mainly because several units must be moved at any time and the state space is usually very large. The planning horizon can be extremely long, where the actions taken at the start of a game affect the overall strategy. In addition, there is the challenge of predicting the moves of one or more opponents, who also have multiple units. RTS are games that do not progress in discrete turns, but where actions can be taken at any time. The RTS games add the challenge of prioritizing time to the already substantial challenges of playing strategy games [1].

AI has been used in RTS games for research and innovation, in particular relying in Deep Learning (DL) topologies [2]. TD is a subgenre of RTS of games and it usually consists of a path where some enemies move and, around that path, the player can position some towers, responsible for causing damage to enemies. Enemies usually come in waves, groups of enemies that hoard together to try to complete the path. If an enemy manages to reach the end of the path, the player is usually punished in some way, such as losing life points, losing overall score or other form of punishment.

The work described in this paper led us through the design and development of a TD game to control the variables needed to research the application of RL for an agent. Also we did not find in the literature another implementation of agents to play *Tower Defense*. The first step is to focus on how to transfer the game state to the agent so that it uses it to perform actions in that environment. Therefore, the construction of the TD is focused on facilitating the provision of data to the agent's *input*.

1.2 Using Reinforcement Learning in Games

Traditionally, RL uses the information on screen (pixels) as the source of processing [6, 7]. More recently, other format of data has been using in some games, as an example, in StarCraft [8, 11].

Some research has been done around *Atari* games to explore RL. In these games, agents often become even better than professional human players, without the need to explicitly code the logic of the game and its rules [9]. In other words, the agent learns by itself just by looking at the *pixels* of the game, the score and the ability to choose an action (activate buttons on a controller) just like a human player would do [9].

Even though the decision making appears to be simple, it hides the difficult task that any player who has ever played a game has probably noticed, which is the process of making instant decisions based on one of a single combination of *pixels* in a large number of possibilities that can appear on the screen at any time. In addition, there is also the chance that the player will find new, creative, situations.

Moreover, game environments are usually only partially observable. This is because the player is forced to make choices based on an indirect representation of the game (the screen) instead of knowing the parameters that govern the logic of the game. Thus, the player does not fully know the environment in which he is inserted. In addition, the actions to be taken by the player are also indirect, since the player's decisions are in terms of buttons to be pressed, not semantic actions in the game [6].

So, the challenge is complex, but definable: how to use the experience of playing a game to make decisions that increase the score and generalize this decision-making process to new situations that didn't happen before [6]?

Deep Q-network (DQN) take advantage of Artificial Neural Network (ANN) to solve this challenge. The architecture can be divided into two parts. First, a series of convolutional layers learns to detect increasingly abstract features of the game's entry screen. Then, a dense classifier maps the set of these features present in the current observation to an output layer with a node for each combination of buttons in the controller [6]. A better representation of this process is shown in Fig. 1. The *input* consists of *pixels*, which are mapped into sensory characteristics that summarize what is being perceived on the screen through convolutional layers. These characteristics are used by later layers that perform the processing and choose the actions to be taken.

We propose a simplified architecture for the agent. Instead of receiving *pixels* as input, we propose to use metadata. These metadata consists of relevant information collected directly in the game. In this way, the sensory mapping shown in Fig. 1, which depends on the processing of a large amount of *pixels*, is replaced by data that is generated by the game itself, significantly reducing the necessary computational power.

2 Implementation

Considering the type of the game, the requirements of the RL agent and the objective of this work, the metadata collected from the game include: *Score*, number of enemies on the screen, money, lives remaining, the construction positions of the towers. The output was composed of actions such as: building a tower in a certain place, doing nothing, upgrade a tower, destroy a tower (Fig. 2).

INPUT

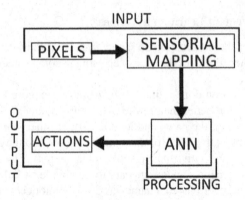

Fig. 1. Simplified model of an agent.

INPUT

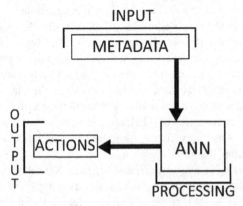

Fig. 2. Suggested model.

This approach has another difference from other works. In TD games there is no real representation of the agent in the world: there is no avatar moving from side to side, taking shots at enemies. Only the results of the actions taken by the agent in the environment are shown, making it impossible to observe which are the places where the agent will build the first towers, which ones he should improve or even destroy. In this work it will be presented only the result of the strategies of the intelligent agent carrying out to reach the final objective of surviving the wave of enemies.

2.1 Tower Defense Project

The software developed was structured into two main modules, the first being TD itself and the second being the agent. As a RTS, the actions taken should be at the game's execution time, making the agent's execution to be in sync.

The TD itself is composed of several parts. The *loop* is responsible for the recognition of the pressed keys, after which comes all the control of the enemies and the towers existing in the game and finally the agent does all its controls, including training the network, generating a *output*.

All the data that comes from the TD can serve as *input* for the agent. However, using too much data for the network input can slow the agent's learning process. Even so, using less data can make the agent never be able to converge, since he does not have enough information to achieve its purpose.

The training process depend on two main factors. The input data and the configuration of the neural network. The variation of the *input* of the network was a common process in this type of work. There were no values, or ideas for what the ideal *input* would look like for the network. In relation to the configuration of the neural network, several changes were made to the hidden layers of the network. Sometimes making it deeper and sometimes more shallow. During the development of the work described in this paper, many configurations were tried.

Initially TD was planned with a number of features, such as global improvements to the towers, slowing down enemies, a chance to apply attacks that would do double or triple damage and a means of restoring life. However, during the development process, it was noticed that several concepts initially foreseen should be abandoned due to the increase in the diversity of plays, so the game was simplified.

In a TD game, the assignment of lives to the player is a means of making the game come to an end. All enemies have an amount of damage that is discounted from lives when they reach the end of the path. The agent has a initial value of 20, and when it reaches zero, the game is over. Moreover, in the context of this work, further simplifications were made, restricting to a single, infinite, wave of enemies that are gradually strengthened. In addition, for progressively increasing the difficulty level, there are two mechanisms. The first is to increase the amount of health of new enemies generated as time passes. The second is to unlock more types of enemies as the agent progresses through the game. Initially only *slimes* are generated and, as time goes by, other enemies are unlocked offering new challenges to the player.

Some definitions that were used to implement the game are:

1. **Enemies:** responsible for the difficulty factor of the game. Each enemy has information such as: the amount of money he gives when he dies, the amount of points he gives when he dies, the amount of life he takes when crossing the defined path, the amount of life he has and the speed at which the enemy moves. Six types of enemies have been created where each has different attribute values.
2. **Path:** where enemies travel, from a starting point to an end point.
3. **Agent:** controls the construction, improvement and sale of the towers. Each of these actions has consequences that may not be immediate, adding to the game's challenge. The agent must take actions considering what he observes in the environment. The agent's goal is to achieve the highest score possible before losing all their lives.
4. **Towers:** responsible for defeating enemies that are walking the path around them. The different types of towers are characterized by information such as the damage done to enemies for each attack it makes, the range of each attack, the price to buy it, the price to make an improvement and the speed at which it executes an attack. The improvement function has been added to the towers, where at a cost of some cash value, the attack range and damage is increased. It is also possible for the towers to be sold, returning part of the money invested in them.

5. **Score:** represents the agent's ability to play the game. The higher the score, the better the agent was able to deal with the situations presented during the game. The score is increased by killing enemies throughout the game.
6. **Money:** resource for building and improving the towers. Money is earned by shooting down enemies or selling towers.
7. **Lives:** number that represents the agent's health. Condition of end of the game.

2.2 Parametrization

As RTS game, a balance is necessary for the game to be fun and offer a fair challenge. Therefore, there was a calibration phase of the game parameters in search of this balance. The game was calibrated in a way that allows a challenge to the human, but that is subject to considerable scoring.

The dimension of the enemies was based on mixing some attributes. Each enemy has a unique characteristic and certain combinations in the generation of enemies would create challenging situations. For example, if some enemies are resistant and resilient (have a lot of life) and slow speed, and are spawned simultaneously with several fast and weak enemies, they could take advantage to get to the end of the path, since the towers would be focused on attacking slow enemies that first entered the tower's reach. Table 1 shows the values given to enemies of TD.

Table 1. List of attributes of each enemy in the TD.

Enemy	Money	Score	Damage	Health base	Move speed
Slime	3	5	1	10	1
Scorpion	10	15	2	20	1.25
Skeleton	5	15	2	15	1.5
Orc	15	30	3	30	0.75
Golem	25	55	5	50	0.5
Flyer	5	15	1	15	2

The definition of the number and characteristics of the towers was defined looking for balance in relation to the enemies. Starting with a balanced tower in its attributes and spawning others with an attribute with a high value and another with a low value. Thus, for each tower there were scenarios in which it fit most efficiently. With this, the agent had several strategies to explore, just varying the combination of the towers and their positions. Table 2 shows the characteristics used by the towers.

The data presented in Table 2 are only the base values for each tower. Performing the improvement in the tower causes some of these parameters to be upgraded, allowing the game to be more balanced for the agent's side. Table 3 presents the data that are added for each improvement made in each type of tower. All towers have a maximum limit of ten improvements.

Table 2. List of attributes of each tower in the TD.

Tower	Base damage	Range	Buy price	Attack speed
Basic	6	125	20	1
Mortar	12	200	30	3
Repeater	2	100	50	0.25

Table 3. Additional values when upgrading the tower.

Tower	Damage	Range	Additional price
Basic	6	5	10
Mortar	12	15	15
Repeater	2	5	25

There are some other responsibilities that have been attributed to the game map, such as generating new enemies. The value for this generation was set at 1.5 s for the graphical version. In addition to generating new enemies, the map is also responsible for gradually increasing the game's difficulty. The difficulty of the game is increased every 30 s.

2.3 Development

The first developed version of the game has a graphical interface, enabling both the agent and a human to play the game. Also during this version, numerous parameter calibrations were made, based on observations of the game.

Figure 3 shows the game screen where it can be seen that there are eight gray dots and three of them are already occupied with towers. These are the possible points at which the player can build the towers. The number of points and the positions of the towers were maintained in all experiments.

In preliminary tests it was observed that each match with graphical interface took a long time to finish, which would prevent the execution of an appropriate amount of tests. Typically, agents trained by RL in gaming environments need several iterations to converge [10]. Therefore, it was necessary to look for an efficient way to simulate the execution of the game, before proceeding with the development of the agent. Matches took a long time to run due to the graphical interface, but also because the game's events were based on the real world clock. The reliance on the clock was necessary for humans to be able to play, allowing the observation and calibration of parameters, making the game balanced and capable of formulating strategies. To make executions faster, the game was reimplemented without the graphical interface. Reliance on the game's real world clock has also been eliminated, for better analysis of the RL training and results.

With this change, TD can be seen as a simulator. In the graphical version, the timing of game events was based on the real world clock. For example, new enemies appeared

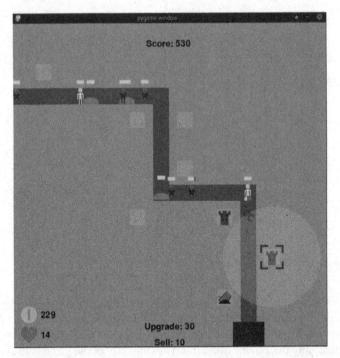

Fig. 3. First version of the game, with a graphical interface.

every 1.5 s from the real world clock. So, no matter how efficient the implementation is, it would be necessary to wait a second and a half for a new enemy to enter the game. Since all the events in the game were tied to the real world clock, this made the execution of a game too long. Although the idea of the simulator is not to depend on the clock in the real world, it is necessary to use some measure of time to synchronize the events that happen in the game. In this way, we call each iteration of the game a *cycle*.

To preserve the balance of the simulated game with the calibration obtained in the graphical version, it was necessary to find a way to map the clock time in cycles. For this, we created a unit called *Epoch*, equivalent to one second of the clock time, which consists of 840 cycles.

The transition from the graphics game to the simulation had to be done using some data as a basis. These data were taken from enemy move speeds and are: 0.5; 0.75; 1; 1.25; 1.5; 1.75 and 2. The first step in working with this data was to find a common value among all these data and with this common value future calculations would not result in float values. In order for all of them to become whole values, each of them was multiplied by four, resulting in the values: 2, 3, 4, 5, 6, 7 and 8. With these new values, a minimum common multiple among all was realized. them, resulting in 840, so every 840 cycles we have an Epoch.

In the first version of the simulator, all cycles were performed. In each cycle, several checks were made to determine if it was time to trigger possible events. However, in the vast majority of cycles there was no event to trigger, which made the checks exhaustive and inefficient. As a result, the total of running time wasn't absurdly lower than in the graphic version of the game.

In a second version of TD without an interface, the idea was to skip cycles that would have no events to run. For this, an execution list was created, where each game object calculated in which cycle the next event would be triggered.

The execution queue consists of a collection of events ordered by the number of cycles until their next execution. The descriptor of each event consists of a tuple containing a reference to the object, the number of cycles until the next execution and the number of cycles between the executions of the events. In the following example, the next event will be triggered by the SLIME_1 object in 10 cycles. This means that it is not necessary to simulate the next 10 cycles as no event will happen. In this way, SLIME_1 triggers its event and 10 cycles are subtracted from the number of cycles for the next execution of all objects in the list. In addition, SLIME_1 is reinserted in the list with 20 cycles remaining until its next run, which corresponds to its period.

```
Queue before SLIME_1 execution:
[[ SLIME_1, 10, 20], [ SCORPION_1, 15, 15], [ BASIC, 420, 840]]
Queue after SLIME_1 execution:
[[ SCORPION_1, 5, 15], [ SLIME_1, 20, 20], [ BASIC, 410, 840]]
```

If an enemy dies, or a tower is sold, these objects are immediately removed from the execution list. When a new tower is purchased or a new enemy is generated, they are placed in the execution list in order.

3 Development of the RL Agent

The development of an intelligent agent using a RL approach is an experimental task. This approach requires careful design of system components such as *inputs*, *outputs* and the learning mechanism. In addition, there are several components in the system that are configurable, which makes it necessary to carry out several experiments to determine the best combinations of parameters.

There would be countless ways to extract the metadata and use them as input for the agent, like the model proposed for the agent, shown in Fig. 2, which had its *input* characterized by metadata taken from TD. So we had to test various combinations of metadata. The next step was the definition of a ANN whose learning mechanism should be able to approximate the Q function. Finally, the end point, where the agent could perform actions in the game such as: construction, improvement and towers sales. We did an exploration looking for different ways to represent the way out.

One of the challenges of agents using DQN is that the neural network used tends to forget previous experiences, as they replace them with new experiences [13]. Therefore, it is necessary to maintain a collection of experiences and observe them to train the model with those previous experiences. This collection of experiences is known as memory.

All the agents implemented in this work had their memory with a defined size of 2000. Each piece of memory consists of:

```
[state, action, reward, next_state, done]
```

State and *next state* are the information the agent has about the environment in the current state and the next state, respectively. Each state represents the agent's entries. *Action* is the action that the agent performed when it was in *state*. *Reward* says how much reward the agent has accumulated between *state* and *next state*. *Done* is used only to inform the end of the game after this action has been taken.

DQN approximates the Q function, which relates a state and an action to the expected reward. To approximate the Q function using a neural network, an error function which can be optimized is necessary. Such a function lists how much a prediction differs from the real value of the function. Equation 1, proposed by [13], presents the error function used in agent training. s is the current state and a is the action taken. s' is the state reached from the action a in state s. a' is the action that maximizes the reward in the s' state. r is the reward between s and s'. The equation is the quadratic error between the prediction $Q(s, a)$, in relation to the value of $r + \gamma\, Q(s'; a')$. In other words, it represents the divergence between the predicted value for the reward when taking the action a in the state s in relation to a precise approximation, obtained after obtaining the reward and forecasting the reward in the next state.

$$loss = r + \gamma \max_{a'} Q\left(s', a'\right) - Q(s, a))^2 \tag{1}$$

Usually, the reward is tied to the score the agent is getting, [4, 13, 14]. In this work we follow this same idea. The reward was considered in three scenarios. Being a periodic reward, a reward linked to enemies and a penalty when the agent loses the game.

3.1 Game Metadata

The metadata taken from the game varied according to the various tests performed. The agent's *input* varied in size and even the form in which the agent's environment was represented.

Table 4 presents some of the information taken from the game and passed to the agent.

The most relevant point is the diversity of combinations that we can provide to the agent. In this work, we explored only some of the possibilities of the various combinations of information in the game. The various combinations directly impact on how the agent observed the environment, consequently its performance as well.

In the first versions of the game, some humans were put to play and we collected the various scores they obtained. In relation to the implemented agents, the average performance obtained was lower than that of the human. However, it is possible to observe an evolution of the score over the various combinations assembled for the agent to observe the environment. This evolution is shown by Table 5.

The average score that a human reached 18680 points, in a few matches the human already managed to reach high scores. However, the agents performed 2309 matches, and during the various combinations the maximum average increased. Also decreasing the difference between maximum score and the mean score. Keeping this pattern, increasing the amount of executions the agent could get results closer to human.

Table 4. Inputs used for agents.

Input size	Input data	
16	Selected tower	Tower type, Tower level
20	General	Lives, Money, Score, difficulty level, Selected tower (8), Enemies amount
	Selected Tower	Tower level (4), Tower type, Upgrade price, Sell refund
65	General	Money
	Each Tower	Enemies killed by type (6), Tower type, Tower level
83	General	Money Enemies by type for one third of path (18)
	Each Tower	Enemies killed by type (6), Tower type, Tower level

Table 5. Scores obtained from agents.

Maximum average	Maximum score
1032,65	8815
1871,25	5505
1518,70	5130
1746,25	5515
1879,65	5305
1981,70	5460
1915,00	6110
1814,50	4935
1940,45	5610
2180,65	5695

4 Conclusion

In this work several agents were developed using Reinforcement Learning techniques based on *Deep Q-Learning* to play *Tower Defense*. In other jobs using *Deep Q-Learning*, agents usually receive video frames from the game as input. In this work we investigate the possibility of the agent receiving metadata from the match as input. As we did not find in the literature another implementation of agents to play *Tower Defense*, the agent was built in an experimental and incremental way.

Initially the game was designed with the aim of encouraging the player to create strategies to overcome the increasingly challenging hordes of enemies. Firstly, the game was implemented with a graphical interface, allowing humans to play. Using this version, the game was calibrated to offer a balance between challenge and fun. Several parameters of the agent were initially adjusted in this version.

As the graphical version was designed for humans to play, the timing of the game's events was dependent on the real world clock. This caused the matches to take a long time to execute. This would prevent long-term experiments, which is important for assessing the trend of the agent's progress. The solution found was to re-implement the game in a version that does not depend on the real world clock and that does not use a graphical interface. This implementation was called a simulated version. All other agents were developed in this new version.

This work showed that it is possible to build an agent based on Reinforcement Learning capable of playing Tower Defense. No other work in the literature reports the development of autonomous agents to learn how to play this type of game. In addition, the design of metadata based inputs made it possible to use input data that is simpler than approaches based on video frames. For this reason, this approach is promising to embed agents based on reinforcement learning in devices with less computational power.

The results reported in this work suggest new directions for future work. The agents used in this work do not directly model the temporal relationship between the sequences of actions and their respective consequences. Future work might include the evaluation of how the use of techniques based on temporal patterns, such as Long short-term memory (LSTM)s and hidden Markov chains can be used to consider temporal behavior. Another possible research would be to evaluate the strategies created by the agent. Strategy evaluation is a technique that can help improve the calibration of parameters in other games. Exploring more input variations for agents is also a possible future work, seeking to provide more relevant information for decision making. Finally, a comparison with an agent based on video frames would also be interesting to assess the difference in performance between this approach and the approach presented in this work.

Acknowledgments. This work has been supported by FCT – Fundação para a Ciência e Tecnologia within the Project Scope: UIDB/05757/2020.

References

1. Justesen, N., Bontrager, P., Togelius, J., Risi, S.: Deep Learning for Video Game Playing. arxiv (2017). https://arxiv.org/pdf/1708.07902.pdf
2. Peng, P., et al.: Multiagent Bidirectionally-Coordinated Nets for Learning to Play StarCraft Combat Games. CoRR (2017). http://arxiv.org/abs/1703.10069
3. Gym library. https://gym.openai.com/. Accessed 16 May 2020
4. Deep Q-Learning with Keras and Gym. https://keon.github.io/deep-q-learning/. Accessed 20 May 2020
5. How to teach AI to play Games: Deep Reinforcement Learning. https://towardsdatascie nce.com/how-to-teach-an-ai-to-play-games-deep-reinforcement-learning-28f9b920440a. Accessed 12 May 2020
6. Advanced DQNs: Playing Pac-man with Deep Reinforcement Learning. https://towardsda tascience.com/advanced-dqns-playing-pac-man-with-deep-reinforcement-learning-3bd99e 0814. Accessed 25 Apr 2020

7. How to match DeepMind's Deep Q-Learning score in Breakout. https://towardsdatascience. com/tutorial-double-deep-q-learning-with-dueling-network-architectures-4c1b3fb7f756. Accessed 25 Oct 2019
8. Justesen, N., Risi, S.: Learning Macromanagement in StarCraft from Replays using Deep Learning. CoRR (2017). https://arxiv.org/pdf/1707.03743.pdf
9. My first experience with deep reinforcement learning. https://medium.com/ai-society/my-first-experience-with-deep-reinforcement-learning-1743594f0361. Accessed 21 Feb 2020
10. Mnih, V., et al.: Playing Atari with Deep Reinforcement Learning. arxiv (2013). https://arxiv. org/pdf/1312.5602v1.pdf
11. Usunier, N., Synnaeve, G., Lin, Z., Chintala, S.: Episodic Exploration for Deep Deterministic Policies: An Application to StarCraft Micromanagement Tasks. CoRR (2016). https://arxiv. org/pdf/1609.02993.pdf
12. Arulkumaran, K., Deisenroth, M.P., Brundage, M., Bharath, A.A.: A Brief Survey of Deep Reinforcement Learning. arxiv (2017). https://arxiv.org/pdf/1708.05866.pdf
13. Mnih, V., et al.: Human-level control through deep reinforcement learning. Nature **518**, 529 (2015)
14. Van Hasselt, H., Guez, A., Silver, D.: Deep reinforcement learning with double q-learning. In: Thirtieth AAAI Conference on Artificial Intelligence (2016)

Author Index

Printed in the United States
by Baker & Taylor Publisher Services